Pursuing Truth, Exercising Power

UNIVERSITY SEMINARS

Leonard Hastings Schoff Memorial Lectures

The University Seminars at Columbia University sponsor
an annual series of lectures, with the support of
the Leonard Hastings Schoff and Suzanne Levick Schoff
Memorial Fund. A member of the Columbia faculty is
invited to deliver before a general audience three lectures
on a topic of his or her choosing. Columbia University Press
publishes the lectures.

David Cannadine
The Rise and Fall of Class in Britain 1993

Charles Larmore
The Romantic Legacy 1994

Saskia Sassen
*Sovereignty Transformed: States and the New
Transnational Actors* 1995

Robert Pollack
*The Faith of Biology and the Biology of Faith: Order,
Meaning, and Free Will in Modern Medical Science* 2000

Ira Katznelson
*Desolation and Enlightenment: Political Knowledge After the
Holocaust, Totalitarianism, and Total War* 2003

Pursuing Truth, Exercising Power

Social Science and Public Policy in the Twenty-first Century

Lisa Anderson

COLUMBIA UNIVERSITY PRESS

NEW YORK

Columbia University Press

Publishers Since 1893

New York, Chichester, West Sussex

Copyright © 2003 Columbia University Press

All rights Reserved

Library of Congress Cataloging-in-Publication Data

Anderson, Lisa

    Pursuing truth, exercising power : social
sciences and public policy in the twenty-first /
Lisa Anderson.

        p.   cm. — (Leonard Hastings Schoff
memorial lectures)

    Includes bibliographical references and index.

    ISBN 0-231-12606-9 (alk. paper)

    1. Policy sciences.   2. Social sciences.

3. Social sciences—United States—History.

4. Privatization.   5. Common good.   I. Title.

II. University seminars/Leonard Hastings Schoff
memorial lectures.

H97.A63 2003

320'.6—dc21

                         2003043834

Design by Brady McNamara

Columbia University Press books are printed on
permanent and durable acid-free paper

Printed in the United States of America

10 9 8 7 6 5 4 3 2 1

To
Samuel Anderson Rauch

and
Isaac Anderson Rauch

Contents

Acknowledgments

This book is a product of enormous generosity, even license, on the part of my family, friends, and colleagues. I am by training and professional formation a political scientist and I have spent most of my career conducting research, writing, and teaching about state formation and political regimes in the Middle East and North Africa. The willingness of the selection committee for the Leonard Hastings Schoff Memorial Lectures to indulge my wish to explore a different set of questions in the 2000 annual lecture series—probably not what they expected when they initially issued the invitation—was one of the first acts of generosity associated with the project.

My interest in the intersection of social science and public policy is a reflection of the contagious enthusiasm for ideas and engagement, for deliberation, and for activism that I have encountered among the students, faculty, and administration of Columbia's School of International and Public Affairs, where I have been dean since 1997. With students from more than 100 countries converging on New York to live and to learn the skills they believe they will need to make the world a better place—more peaceful, more prosperous, more sustainable, more just—SIPA has provided me, as it does its students, an excellent education in the challenges and opportunities that will confront policymakers today and tomorrow. That so many of the School's faculty attended the lectures on which this book is based, read the manuscript, warned me away from errors, and pointed me toward more interesting ideas is a remarkable testament to the generosity of those associated with the institution. The School's administrators, particularly Patrick Bohan, Robin Lewis, Joan Turner and, as always, Jo Leondopoulos, graciously afforded me time to work on these ideas virtually (although, thankfully, not entirely) undisturbed. Marc, Sam, and Isaac Rauch were also generous in the many and varied distractions they provided at home and for that I am immeasurably grateful.

Strictly speaking, this is not a work of social science research nor is it really policy analysis, although it draws on social science and advocates public policies. As such it builds on the work of my fellow social scientists and I am happily indebted to those, particularly the historians and sociologists, whose work has provided the material from which I have so liberally drawn in fashioning my arguments. I hope these arguments lead them to consider the significance of their work in new ways. Similarly, although this is not a work of policy analysis or advocacy in any conventional sense, I hope that it contributes to a debate about how we define the role of the university in the public sphere and how we equip public policymakers in the twenty-first century.

Among those who bear some specific responsibility for what intelligence this book exhibits are Hisham Aidi, Jon Anderson, Said Amir Arjomand, Peter Bearman, Robert Belknap, Leslie Bialler, Sheila Biddle, Anissa Bouziane, Craig Calhoun, Charles

Cameron, Douglas Chalmers, Steven Cohen, Dennis Dijkzeul, Paul Evans, Ester Fuchs, F. Gregory Gause, C. Lowell Harris, Eric Hershberg, J. C. Hurewitz, Ira Katznelson, Robert Legvold, William MacAllister, Mahmood Mamdani, David Maurrasse, Anthony Marx, Elsbieta Matynia, Mary McDonnell, Robert K. Merton, Roberta Balstead Miller, James W. Morley, Andrew J. Nathan, Richard R. Nelson, Neema Noori, Kenneth Prewitt, Azzedine Rakkah, Marc Rauch, Robert Y. Shapiro, Gary Sick, Stephen Solnick, David Stark, Frank and Jackie Stehlick, Anders Stephanson, Leslie Vinjamuri, Robert Vitalis, David Waldner, Kent Worcester, and the late Aaron Warner. As always, none of these people is responsible for the errors and infelicities I have insisted on retaining.

Lisa Anderson
February 2003

Pursuing Truth, Exercising Power

1

Introduction

*Understanding, Intervention,
and the Common Good*

This book explores the relationship between social science and
public policy at the dawn of the twenty-first century. In many respects, that century opened with the shock of the terrorist attacks of September 11, 2001. In New York City, as the cloudless
September sky filled with smoke and ashes, we confronted both
our wish to comprehend what had happened and our need to do
something constructive in the face of the devastation in our
midst. Those two desires—to understand and to act—shaped
the months that followed, revealing for all to see both how intimate and how fragile are the connections between the domains
of social science and public policy.

From the New York City Office of Emergency Management,
which mobilized to support rescue and recovery, to the broker-
age firms who reconstituted their trading floors in Jersey City,
from the National Security Council, which coordinated the US
response in the "war on terrorism," to the Red Cross which organized support for families of victims—public, not-for-profit,

and private policymakers responded, operating on the basis of the accumulation of best practices, academic research, job training, and guesswork. At the same time, scholars and intellectuals across the United States, called upon to explain what had happened and what should be done, exhibited a perhaps surprising, perhaps becoming, reluctance to debate these responses, mobilizing instead to understand—organizing forums on the rebuilding of lower Manhattan, mining research on Afghanistan, assembling teams to collect oral histories among the survivors. Ill-disposed, or maybe just ill-equipped, to address the enormity of the implications of September 11 and the nation-wide tide of patriotism that became the emblem of community and condolence, social scientists seemed to find solace and relief in research that would answer if not the questions of the moment, perhaps those of tomorrow.

These varied reactions illustrated what had long been apparent, that the relationship between scholars and practitioners, between social science and public policy, is one of simultaneous fascination and exasperation. Social scientists are often dismissive of the lack of analytical rigor that typifies the conduct of public policy—the need to act before all the answers are known—while policy practitioners are bemused by the theoretical pretensions of social science—the reluctance to act in the absence of all the answers. Yet there is a mutual expectation among scholars and practitioners that, if only each would recognize the merits, the culture, the demands of the other's domain, science and policy would both be better for it.

I have puzzled over this awkward and sometimes disheartening relationship both before and after September 11 from my particularly favored vantage point as dean of Columbia University's School of International and Public Affairs. This institution has the uncommon aspect of a school of public policy embedded in a faculty of arts and sciences and the responsibility of its management has allowed—indeed, required—me to spend much of my time considering how best to marshal the social sciences in preparing policy analysts and managers for the world they will encounter as professionals. This I have done in the belief not only that public policy will be enhanced by such exposure to social science but also that closer familiarity with the challenges that face policymakers is salutary for social science itself.

As I have pondered this relationship, I have come to realize that it contains far more tension and ambiguity even than we ordinarily acknowledge. The dual aspiration to understand and to change the world of which early modern social science was born marked it with a profound ambivalence about power and policy. The story of the development of the social sciences is a story of repeated oscillations between the embrace of active, indeed assertive, participation in policymaking, and retreat into the ostensibly neutral posture of scientific objectivity. This ambivalence about policy in the practice of science—the divorce of truth from power—is a distinctly American element of the story of the rise of the social sciences. Born as handmaidens of democracy and industrial capitalism in the formation of the American state, the social sciences soon relinquished this definition of their purpose to pursue an agenda that seemed to be at once more abstract and more inclusive. In creating the illusion that truth and power are separable domains, social scientists claimed the pursuit of truth as their own and relegated the exercise of power to "practitioners." This diluted and complicated the role social scientists would play in the development of democracy and capitalism in the United States but, thanks to the conceit that these "sciences" were in essence apolitical, this illusion also contributed to the enormous influence that American versions of social science would have in the rest of the world.

The conditions that shaped the rise and expansion of American social science are rapidly changing, however, and with them, the terms of its relationship with power and policy. By the end of the twentieth century, public policy was less and less associated with its classic locus in government. It was now made and implemented by consultants and firms in the private sector, by not-for-profits and NGOs, by transnational and community-based organizations alike. Leverage for action that defined "the good" and benefitted "the public" was no longer located only in government. Moreover, all of these organizations and movements were spreading around the world in ways that paid only partial deference to existing institutions. Multinational firms were playing havoc with national trade statistics, as they transferred goods and services from branches in multiple sovereign jurisdictions without ever buying or selling anything. Transnational advocacy networks linked local community groups across the globe; from Human Rights Watch to Slumdwellers International, local concerns are projected onto world screens.

These trends, captured crudely in the notions of privatization and globalization, were not unrelated. They both constituted challenges to, perhaps even renunciations of, the primacy of the state in shaping social life both locally and globally, a primacy which has characterized the last several centuries. Because the events of September 11 revealed a dark side to globalization and privatization—the criminal conspiracies of trade in drugs and people, money-laundering and arms smuggling, that supported, among other things, international terrorist networks—they contributed to decelerating these trends, but not to their reversal. The Bush Administration modulated its hostility to "big government" to enhance what it called homeland security, but it continued to advocate diminishing the role of government in most realms of American life. Indeed, in the same week Congress authorized the creation of the new Department of Homeland Security, the Bush Administration announced plans to privatize as many as 850,000 government jobs, almost half the federal civilian work force.[1] Similarly, the Administration's unilateralist impulses and resistance to international institutions in pursuit of the "war on terrorism" were constrained by virtually unanimous support among other governments and NGOs around the world for supra-national institutions like the United Nations.

The challenge posed to the primacy of the state by privatization and globalization was not limited to the creation of new demands and opportunities for public policy; it also raised important questions about the future of the social sciences, since they were born in the service of the modern state, and they evolved in a way that left them quite closely, if often invisibly, tied to the purposes and institutions of states, particularly liberal states like that of the United States. If we remove the state or, perhaps better, if we complicate its role as the point of contact between the social sciences and public policy, how will they interact? How have the ideas, the assumptions, the methods of the social sciences permeated our cultures and societies? How does widespread, if often unselfconscious, adoption of social scientific approaches shape the formulation of policy beyond government? And what of the cultures and societies in which social science is nearly as foreign as the state itself? How will the dissemination of social science—its globalization—shape public policy in those societies? Finally, how will the changing contours of public policy shape in turn the character of social science research?

I begin with some reflections on the history of social science and public policy in the United States where, as I hope to show, a very particular—even peculiar—relationship between the social sciences and public policy evolved with the growth of the modern welfare state and American ascension to world power. The social sciences that reflect this peculiar relationship were disseminated around the world in the second half of the twentieth century, giving apparent support to their claims of universality. Yet, the social and political world in which the modern institutions of social research and policy originated was fast disappearing, transformed by global changes in information technologies, social organizations, and individual aspirations. The significance of the state in both making public policy and supporting social science—one might even say, in defining the "public" and the "social" and distinguishing truth from power—was supplemented by alternative locations of authority and innovation. I examine the significance of this change for the character of the social sciences and their relationship to public policy in the second chapter. The additional challenges posed by the globalization of the social sciences—by the apparent realization of their universalist ambitions—to both public policy and the social sciences themselves are the subject of the third chapter.

Ultimately, I believe that this story represents yet another chapter in the at once foreign and familiar story of the liberal order. The ideas and the institutions which animate and support social science research reflect a historically and cultural specific commitment to a sort of traditional American liberalism, one that was simultaneously skeptical of and reliant upon the state, unselfconscious in its embrace of the rhetoric of equality and the reality of privilege, and supremely confident in the susceptibility of social problems to human intervention. Taken together and rarely examined, these ideas allowed the flowering of a remarkable intellectual project over the last century. It is, however, an armature unlikely to be sustained in the face of the challenges posed by the new entrants in the formulation, advocacy, and management of the policies which will shape our world in the next decades. It is to consideration of this challenge that I return at the end of this essay.

2

A Science of Politics

*The American History of Scientific Policy
and Policy-Making*

In 1880, John W. Burgess established the first graduate school of
political science in the United States at Columbia University.
This school, originally proposed as a School for Preparation for
the Civil Service, was, as the university president put it,

> designed to prepare men for public life, whether in the Civil
> Service at home or abroad, or in the legislatures of the states or
> the nation; and also to fit young men for the duties and re-
> sponsibilities of public journalists.[1]

Almost exactly a hundred years later, in 1978, the bulletin of Columbia's brand-new Graduate Program in Public Policy and Administration announced that its objective was

> to train men and women to analyze, develop, administer, and
> evaluate public policies and programs. . . . Policy-making, ad-
> ministrative and advisory positions suited for graduates . . . will

be found in executive and legislative branches of central city, suburban, state and federal levels of government. . . . [2]

What happened in the years that intervened between these two announcements—apart from the addition of women to public life and a palpable deterioration in rhetorical style—is the subject of this chapter. Why has preparing men and women for public life by exposing them to graduate education in the social sciences seemed like a good idea? Twice? Why did Burgess's experiment fail? Why did the university try again? And, more generally, why, despite this apparently checkered history, do American educators continue to believe that social science should be associated with the training of public servants?

To some, the answers to these questions may be simple. After all, Robert Merton warned us nearly sixty years ago that "the honeymoon of intellectuals and policy-makers is often nasty, brutish and short."[3] Yet there is ample evidence that, despite repeated disappointments, the lovers remain infatuated.

THE MODERN STATE AND THE
SCIENCE OF SOCIETY

Many elements of the relationship, including many of the tensions, reflect a particularly, if not uniquely, American history of state-formation and social transformation. Just as American liberalism shaped the development of the American state, it defined the organization of the social sciences and their relationship to public policy.[4] Indeed, it is fair to say that the institutions Americans devised to confront the challenges of authority and innovation over the last century include the social sciences themselves.

Modern social inquiry was born in the development of the modern state. Philosophers have certainly offered observations on the public good and on ways rulers might serve the commonweal since time immemorial. All scholars of international relations pay obeisance to Thucydides; all students of government acknowledge Machiavelli. That we return to *The Peloponnesian Wars* and *The Prince* is a testament to the universality of some of the dilemmas policymakers face—as well, of course, to the remarkable insight and eloquence of their authors—but there is much in the modern world that has changed the relationship between the domain of reflection and inquiry and that of public life. Statistics, as the word itself suggests, were originally data collected by rulers to aid them in carrying out the affairs of government. As the European state of the sixteenth and seventeenth century grew more autonomous and capable, and as intermediate organizations—churches and guilds, manors and towns—gave way in the face of its ambitions, information itself was transformed. Whether in censuses, cadastral surveys, tax rolls, public health records, or crime statistics, information became more abstract, more formal, more "stylized," as we say, and more useful. Society became, as James Scott put it, more "legible," and the availability of these statistics permitted readers to "discover new social truths as well as merely summarizing known facts."[5]

The modern state and its instruments reflected not only a new approach to information but also, soon enough, a novel conception of the purpose of government. Indeed, as Desrosieres suggests, there is a historical and conceptual link between political and moral ideas about equity and statistical and scientific notions of equivalence: "at first, the comparability and the equivalence between objects were less questions of knowledge than of justice."[6] As sovereignty slipped from the crown to the people, what had been an apparatus serving the ruler slowly expanded and transformed into a public bureaucracy, a civil service, whose purpose was not only to monitor but also to enhance the welfare of society. As Scott put it, "the existing social order . . . was for the first time the subject of active management."[7] This produced deliberate *policy* on the part of state officials charged with managing the affairs of state and—importantly—of the public.[8]

Today policy exists everywhere: a firm's statement on corporate benefits, a school's dress code, a supermarket's prohibition of bare feet are all designed to provide clear guidance to employees, students, or customers about how the institution intends to provide compensation, maintain decorum, ensure cleanliness. Because it originated in the ambitions of the modern state, *public* policy is associated with that state: it has customarily been formulated and implemented by governments, in the public sector. That association is not definitive, however, for policy whose intended recipient is "the public" may also be made by individuals and groups who are not in government. Indeed, in examining both the eras before and after the rise of the welfare state we must be careful not to equate public policy with its institutional or sectoral origin but rather define it by its purpose or end. As Walter Powell has suggested, we can ask whether "the goals and interests of organizations and their leaders and managers are congruent with the interests of the larger society such that the activities of the organizations . . . increase the collective well-being of society."[9]

Many American students of public policy, accustomed as they are to a democratic institutional environment, are profoundly uncomfortable with this extension of public policy beyond government because it complicates the question of accountability. In theory, at least, governments are either elected officials or responsible to such officials, and therefore they are accountable to "the public" they serve. In practice, however, the accountability of even democratic governments is complicated by complex and conflicting institutions and interests and, of course, governments even purporting to be democratic are hardly universal. Indeed, much of the world's "public" is as well served by international organizations, local business, even multinational corporations as they are by their own governments. As Anthony Cordesman recently remarked about the Middle East, for example, "a great deal of the explanation," of the poor performance of the region, "lies in the fact that many Middle Eastern states have no enemy greater than their own governments."[10] Good, effective public policy may be, but has not always been, formulated and implemented by governments.

By the eighteenth century, the locus of what we would call public policy was still quite varied as churches, guilds, trade networks, and tribes worked on behalf of their adherents, members and dependents but the desire of rulers for new and more exact knowledge about their subjects, and about the world around them, provided incentives for new kinds of systematic study. Early modern science was at first pursued almost wholly outside existing universities, which were still the preserve of religious education. The royal academies of Britain and later Napoleon's *grandes écoles,* for example, supported natural science and fostered the search for social knowledge and technological innovation associated with Europe's global expansion. Soon enough, however, the medieval universities of Europe took up new subjects, expanding from schools of theology to include in their missions the creation and dissemination of knowledge about the natural and social world.

As they emerged in the nineteenth century, the social sciences were considered variants of, or analogous to, the natural sciences—only the realm of inquiry was thought to differ.[11] Social philosophers took the natural sciences as the model of inquiry to which they aspired. In France Auguste Comte advocated what he called "social physics;" in England the Benthamites developed their utilitarian calculus. As they evolved, however, the social sciences would prove to be quite different from the natural sciences. Indeed, as J. S. Mill was to argue, "Laws of mind and laws of matter are so dissimilar in their nature that it would be contrary to all principles of rational arrangement to mix them as part of the same study."[12]

In part this difference reflects the fact that what social scientists study is shaped by their own imaginative construction; as Peter Hall reminds us, "the economy is not visible to the naked eye: it consists in a complex network of human relations and material flows. Thus what we think of as the economy is, in fact, an artifact of current economic science. . . . "[13] These artifacts are choices, and they are shaped by normative preferences. Many of us are so comfortably situated within the prevailing normative order that we never actually make a self-conscious choice among artifacts or perspectives. Yet even the most disengaged technicians in the ranks of the social sciences exhibit the influence of the social world around them in their choice of research terrains and problems. As Whitley argues, it is the nature of the stakeholders—their "everyday concerns and audiences, and a consequent plurality of standards and goals"—that distinguish the social from the natural sciences.[14]

Moreover, unlike the natural sciences, which have often produced findings that go begging for useful application, social scientific findings are routinely born of necessity. The natural scientist has had a question; the social scientist has wanted an answer. The U.S. National Science Foundation's contrast of "development" and "applied research" illuminates this distinction. "Development," the foundation tells us, is the "systematic use of the knowledge or understanding gained from research, directed toward the production of useful materials, devices, systems or methods, including design and development of prototypes and processes." This need to find uses—as opposed to "applied research," which, the NSF tells us, is devoted to "meeting a recognized need"—was an important engine of the expansion of American consumer society in the twentieth century, and it would shape much of the American government's conception of the role of science, and of investment in science, in society.[15] But we get ahead of ourselves.

During the nineteenth century, the American embrace of social inquiry promoted its association with science. While in absolutist France, for example, politics and administration were considered state monopolies, not to be subject to intellectual inquiry or speculation,[16] for Americans, science seemed to support the cause of liberalism, by breaking the yoke of tradition, questioning authority, and celebrating the individual, both as citizen and, ultimately, as what we have come to know as "unit of analysis." Liberalism in turn supported the pursuit of science; freedom of belief, assembly, and association were important prerequisites to unfettered inquiry. After the Civil War, these complementary interests converged in the explosive growth of secular education. Sixty-seven land grant colleges were established throughout the country and the modern American research university began to take shape. The spirit of the time was captured in the observation by Francis Walker, an economist who served as Superintendent of the Census in 1870, that "we must regard liberty no longer as a female but as a fact."[17]

THE GROWTH OF THE AMERICAN UNIVERSITY
AND THE DEVELOPMENT OF THE DISCIPLINES

The association of the American universities with the country's growing liberal and capitalist interests not only fostered a particular approach to social inquiry—what we know today as "methodological individualism"—but also fueled rapid expansion of higher education, which in turn provided receptive audiences and gainful employment for social scientists. Although many in the first generation of academic reformers in the United States studied in Europe, particularly Germany, the terrain that greeted them upon their return was far more open than in Europe itself. Not surprisingly, the liberal cast of American social research found competition in Europe, notably the social inquiry associated with socialism, which also challenged tradition but privileged class over the individual as its methodological building block. Neither liberals nor their competitors found European universities welcoming, however, for entrenched interests slowed university growth and discouraged innovation. In Europe, social inquiry remained closely associated with philosophy and history; in the United States, where there was so little reason to defer to history, social research was free to emulate that most modern of intellectual pursuits, natural science.[18]

Although the sciences, natural and social, were fast transforming higher education, the religious purposes of the original universities of Europe were still powerful influences. In the United States this was expressed less in sectarian or dogmatic terms than in the common conviction that higher education should contribute to the moral improvement of society.[19] Only nine years before Burgess established Columbia's School of Political Science, for example, Columbia's president urged that "that every student be instructed in the important subject of the foundations of religion."[20] Still, he and his counterparts were fast abandoning religious instruction as the mechanism by which their institutions would fulfill their moral mission in favor of a marriage of high-minded concern for the public good with the new scientific temperament.

Thus, from the very outset, social science in the United States was justified by and celebrated for its intimate association with the devotion to moral improvement and the liberal purposes so characteristic of American public policy. As Jean Bethke Elshtain points out, "In the minds of such thinkers as William James, George Herbert Mead and John Dewey, there was no way to separate intellectual and political concerns from larger moral concerns."[21] The American Social Science Association (ASSA) was founded in 1865 by social reformers from government and charitable organizations together with university-based academics.[22] Because reform of the universities was associated with a larger agenda of social reform during the second half of the nineteenth century, however, and because universities were growing so fast, university-based social scientists soon began to concentrate their energies less on direct action on behalf of societal reform and more on the education of public servants and social activists. Over the course of time their active involvement in the political debates of the day diminished in favor of institution-building within their universities. In the 1880s, shortly after John Burgess established his school of political science, Johns Hopkins, Stanford and the University of Chicago, new universities themselves, all inaugurated experimental programs in the social sciences designed for public servants.

Perhaps ironically, this growth in university programs created an academic job market which captured the graduates of the programs themselves. Although Theodore Roosevelt was one of the first graduates of John Burgess's School of Political Science at Columbia, and Woodrow Wilson published scientific studies of administration in the 1880s, ultimately their combination of academic training with public service proved to be the exception. Most of the early graduates of the Columbia Faculty of Political Science or, as it became later, the Graduate School of Arts and Sciences, found employment not in government, but in the expanding universities themselves.[23] Soon enough, highly specialized professional orientations were expressed in the creation of new professional associations, as the ASSA splintered into organizations like the National Council of Charities and Corrections, on one hand, and the American Economic Association, which was founded in 1885, on the other.

By the turn of the twentieth century, the social science disciplines we know today were well on their way to institutionalization. Perhaps not surprisingly, economics was the first of the modern social science disciplines to distinguish itself, as it superseded the "political economy" favored throughout most of the nineteenth century. The abandonment of the political reflected a growing conviction that economic behavior was less a response to historically specific, socially constructed institutions than the reflection of a universal individual psychology whose workings were accessible to modern science.[24]

Although it was consistent with the universalist ambitions of liberalism, this shift in the focus of economics was a more radical departure than it might first appear. If the sources, regularities, causes, and effects of economic behavior were to be discovered in nature, like the workings of the solar system, rather than shaped by institutional structures amenable to intervention, economists might still be useful to policymakers, but in a novel role. Now they were experts who understood the unseen workings of an abstraction known as the market rather than specialists knowledgeable about the social and moral problems of the day. Truth was now invariant, abstract, universal, and power and policy were merely responses or reactions to the truths scientists were to discover. For American liberalism, the assumption of the existence of discoverable regularities in social behavior was an affirmation of its abstract and formal egalitarianism and individualism, and it was quickly embraced as entirely consistent with nineteenth- and early-twentieth-century capitalism. Within the universities, this turn not only privileged scientific methods over history as a basis for social inquiry, it also imposed a distance between science and policy. Moral education and public service were no longer the immediate purpose of social inquiry so much as a happy byproduct.

In its concern with the social consequences of modernity, American sociology reflected its origins in social reform movements. The editor of the *American Journal of Sociology*, Albion Small, wrote in introducing the first issue in 1895 that the contributors would "express their best thoughts upon discoverable principles of societary relationships, in such a way that they might assist all intelligent men in taking the largest possible view of the rights and duties as citizens."[25] Like economics, sociology would adopt a positivist perspective that distinguished it from social work and gave it the air of science. Political science remained more closely allied with the older disciplines of law, philosophy, and history but it too began to emerge as a distinct enterprise at the end of the century, partly in reaction to the development of economics. The abandonment of political economy left politics as a residue, and in suggesting that the state and the market operate by distinctive logics, created a domain for a separate science of politics. Political science retained a formalistic, institutional orientation, however, and abandoned its link to training practitioners more slowly than its sister disciplines, concentrating on the technical aspects of administration and the institutions of democracy.[26]

Early-twentieth-century economics, sociology and, to a lesser extent. political science did, however, find common cause in relegating history to a separate discipline, since they were about *now*—a universal, scientific, transcendent present. History held no intrinsic interest or, more important, explanatory power, and was useful only insofar as its examples confirmed the universality of the laws these sciences seemed to be rapidly uncovering. So too, economics, sociology, and political science were about *here*, about the societies of the scientists themselves, shaped by the growth of the modern state, liberal government, and industrial capitalism. That there were other economic, social, and political forms was acknowledged only by their unapologetic relegation to anthropology.27 The concern with other times and places that characterized history and anthropology meant that these disciplines remained guests in the scientific study of society, too devoted to the particular, the specific, the local to be full members but important repositories nonetheless of what would otherwise have been very inconvenient "data sets."

These new sciences very quickly spawned university departments and professional associations. The American Political Science Association (APSA) was founded in 1903 and two years later, the American Sociological Society (ASS) was established. The APSA reflected the dueling interests of its members: its charter insisting that it would not "assume a partisan position upon any question of politics" while the establishment of the Association journal, *The American Political Science Review*, two years later was heralded as helping bring the discipline "into a position of authority as regards practical politics."28 Social work practitioners were welcome as members of the ASS as long as they had a "scientific" interest in sociology but the rising professional standing of academically based social scientists was fast distancing them from their practitioner counterparts. The new universities and university departments offered stable careers, professional status, and intellectual autonomy: no longer did those who conducted social research have to rely on newspapers, governments, political organizations, or charities for gainful employment—a marked difference from their European colleagues of the day.[29]

The consolidation of the social sciences as disciplines and departments fostered engagement with the social issues of the day on a new footing. Scientific specialization and development of social sciences disciplines had accompanied the relinquishing of the responsibility for moral education by American universities. As empirically based, statistically grounded "value-free" social science came to represent the model of disciplinary rigor, ethics and morality were related to matters of personal preference.

Under the wide sky of liberalism, technocratic expertise replaced moral commitment as the vehicle linking social inquiry and public policy. The Progressive-era reforms at home and expanding American power abroad provided opportunities for university-based social scientists to provide expert advice and consultation to a growing government. As then university professor Woodrow Wilson wrote in 1887, "the idea of the state and the consequent idea of its duty are undergoing noteworthy change. . . . Seeing everyday new things which the state ought to do, the next thing is to see clearly how it ought to do them."[30] Professional demographers were actively involved in the creation of the Bureau of the Census in 1902, for example, and in 1910, political scientist Frank Goodnow went to China to advise the new regime there at the behest of the Carnegie Endowment for International Peace. Economists and psychologists played important roles in government service in World War I; indeed it was during the Great War that the first IQ tests were developed.[31]

This model of the engagement of social researchers with public policy as scientists distinguished the United States from Europe at the time.[32] In intellectual terms, the American liberal lack of interest in the state was early apparent, while the importance of race was enormous. Indeed, as Robert Vitalis has pointed out, the rise of the state in both domestic American politics and social science and in policy and scholarship about the rest of the world during the interwar period replaced and largely obscured an earlier focus on race. The first international affairs journal in the United States, which began publishing in 1910 and would ultimately be taken over by the new Council on Foreign Relations in the 1920s to become the house organ, *Foreign Affairs*, was the *Journal of Race Development*.

As the premier volume of the *Journal of Race Development* makes clear, the boundaries we draw today between what is inside and outside the national territorial space and that are now distinct domains of expertise were not made in the same way in 1910. Perhaps more accurately, who is inside and who is outside the national space was not so much a territorial question as it was a biological one.[33]

In Europe, the long shadow of the state was apparent both in the institutions of social science education and research and in the intellectual preoccupations. Reformist impulses, while important in other realms of social life, did not produce significant changes in higher education, for example, which was to deprive social researchers of the stable careers and intellectual autonomy their American counterparts enjoyed.

In Germany, where so many of the founders of the American social sciences had studied at mid-century, some elements of what would become the characteristically American pattern were evident. German universities combined scientific research and higher education but, in contrast to the developing American system, the post-1870 German university reforms were a state initiative and the German universities remained closely associated with state policy. In France, the role of state sponsorship was even more debilitating. As Heilbron observes,

> despite numerous initiatives, at least from the beginning of the eighteenth century, a school for political or administrative sciences was not founded until almost a century after the Revolution. The political sciences were not only granted no academic rights, the training of civil servants remained equally under the immediate control of the authorities. The creation of a "school," even a purely professional school, would have meant the recognition of certain autonomy. [34]

In 1871, after the Franco-Prussian War, the *Ecole libre des sciences politiques* was established but it was principally devoted to training civil servants and did not foster social research; it would not be linked to the national university system until after World War II. The *grandes écoles* did not develop a research tradition, and the association of research and teaching characteristic of Germany and later the United States remained weak in France.

When John Burgess returned from studying in Germany in the early 1870s, he intended to combine the German university's dedication to public purposes with the French *Ecole libre's* independence of government control, creating what he called "a private institution with a public purpose."[35] This he attempted not only in the establishment of Columbia's Faculty of Political Science but also in founding the journal *Political Science Quarterly* in 1885—still today one of the few journals that reaches audiences of both social scientists and policy practitioners. It was in the second volume of that journal that Woodrow Wilson argued that the existing "science of administration" was a "foreign science . . . developed by French and German professors" and "to answer our purposes, it must be adapted. . . . if we employ it we must Americanize it."[36]

And Americanize it they did, while in Europe the universities played a less and less prominent role in developing social research. Throughout the continent, the sociological insights of Durkheim and Weber found relatively limited audiences within the conservative university systems while in England, for example, academic economics would not make its mark on British government policy until well after World War I,[37] and sociology was not even a recognized discipline until after World War II. Anthropology flourished in shadow of the British Empire, as much a pastime of the colonial officer as the university don, while everywhere in Europe the study of politics remained identified with the law well past the middle of the twentieth century. Social inquiry in Europe was far more closely associated with history and philosophy, as well as with active engagement in public debate. Indeed, thanks in no small measure to the closed ranks of the university systems of Britain and Germany, nonacademic research and writing was typical of the social researchers associated with the movements of the left.

Thus, newspapers, political parties, and government bureaucracies continued to provide employment to social theorists in Europe long after their American counterparts had retreated into a large and welcoming ivory tower. Authority and influence rested less on the scientific expertise than on age-old claims of privilege and of the moral superiority associated with it, as Harold Lasswell found when he visited England in 1923. There, he said, the "academicians have a sense of power. . . . In politics they find the boys they knew at Oxford or at the Settlement [and they meet them] at dinner parties, club lounges, weekends." By contrast, in the United States, he went on, the academy was "scattered over three thousand miles . . . lacking traditions of Lord and Professor . . . relatively impotent . . ."[38]

Lasswell's perhaps surprising intimation of anxiety about the influence of social science reflects more than the absence of connections or cronies; it marks the first indication that the evolving model of the relation between social science and public policy in the United States was unstable. The crux of the matter was that the science these social researchers practiced was, in fact, different from that of their colleagues in the natural sciences. In all science, the orientation to the creation of new and better understanding ensures, as Whitley points out, that "intellectual obsolescence is built in to the knowledge production system" and therefore all scientists labor in a field characterized by more "task uncertainty than in most other vocations."[39] For social scientists, this uncertainty is exacerbated because, as Sheldon Wolin famously observed, natural scientists do not criticize nature. The capacity of social scientists to exercise critical judgment shapes both the scientists' perception of society and society itself.[40] As a result, as Merton put it, "there is a considerable degree of *indeterminacy* in the social scientist's findings, insofar as they bear upon projected action." The competence of social science experts is difficult to assess and their advice is easy to ignore, for not only are their findings indeterminate, as their research subjects change in response to research itself, but those findings also have what Merton called "immediate and obvious value implications."[41] Social scientists were beginning to fear that they had neither the authority of the natural scientist's exactness and objectivity nor the legitimacy of the policymaker's commitment to moral improvement and the public good.[42]

Nonetheless, during the first decades of the twentieth century the contours of a relationship between social science and public policy that would be sustained for nearly a century in the United States were outlined. Demand for university education continued to grow, ensuring the consolidation of disciplinary university-based employment for social scientists. Between 1890 and 1940, the percentage of college-age students attending colleges or universities rose from 2 to 15 percent, securing the revenues and the consumer base of higher education.[43] What was missing was support for the increasingly ambitious and expensive research establishment social scientists sought to locate at the universities. The absence of an explicit public service mission both permitted the science-like stance of social inquiry and accorded well with American liberalism's suspicion of the state, but it also threatened to render social science not just impotent, as Lasswell feared, but penniless.

THE APPEARANCE OF THE PRIVATE FOUNDATIONS

As it happened, yet another uniquely American character appeared in the story of the social sciences and public policy just in time to rescue and prolong the project of liberal science: the large private foundation. There was already a long American tradition of philanthropy, and well before World War I charitable organizations in the United States had supported social welfare projects. In the 1920s, new and immensely rich foundations looked beyond their traditional role, seeking new activities which would be forward-looking and modern, while remaining uncontroversial.[44] Social science research seemed to fit the bill. The Russell Sage and Carnegie Foundations participated in launching the National Bureau of Economic Research in the early 1920s; in 1923, the Laura Spelman Rockefeller Memorial underwrote the establishment of the Social Science Research Council and, with Carnegie, supported the young Brookings Institution in the mid-1920s.

Each of these initiatives reflected the tenacity with which the discipline-based, university-housed model of social science had taken hold within the space of only a few decades. If social science was not adequately serving the public interest, that would be addressed not by rethinking the nature of social inquiry or the social science disciplines but by strengthening the science itself. As the then head of the Laura Spelman Rockefeller Memorial said, "All who work toward the general end of social welfare are embarrassed by the lack of knowledge that the social sciences provide. It is as though engineers were at work without an adequate development in the sciences of physics or chemistry." [45] In their own estimation, the founders of NBER, SSRC, and Brookings were the physicists for whom the engineers of democracy had been waiting. The objectivity and expertise of the social sciences could be reconciled with unembarrassed commitment to the growing welfare state under the banner of liberalism in part because the private foundations were prepared to subsidize scientific research. As Kent Worcester points out, the advantages were thought to be mutual: the founders of the SSRC "contended that social planning through coordinated government action was central to the task of reforming and modernizing society. . . . It also perhaps, sprang from the recognition that informed participation in the national policy environment could enhance the legitimacy of the social sciences." [46]

DEPRESSION, WAR AND THE MOBILIZATION OF SOCIAL SCIENCE

By the end of the 1920s, many of the private foundations began to turn their attention toward medicine, public health, and child development—areas thought to be just as uncontroversial as social science research but more likely to have a demonstrable impact on the improvement of society. The funding and legitimacy crisis for the social sciences this might have entailed was averted by the same mechanism that ensured employment for millions of non-social scientists during the Great Depression and World War II as well—the intervention of the federal government. Although the universities were reluctant to accept government funding of research, concerned that they would lose their prized autonomy, federal support of students began during this period and, more importantly, many faculty served as individuals in the expanding government enterprise. Columbia alone provided Raymond Moley, Rexford Tugwell, and Adolf A. Berle, Jr. to Franklin Roosevelt's famed "Brain Trust" and social scientists joined the government in large numbers, as the embrace of the welfare state and the social sciences tightened dramatically. [47]As Desrosieres puts it,

> The establishment of federal systems of monetary, banking, budgetary, or social regulation gave the government in Washington an entirely new role. To fulfill this new role the administration relied ever more heavily on experts in the social sciences, economics, demographic sociology and law, mainly through the agency of wealthy private foundations: Carnegie, Ford, and Rockefeller. During this period, close ties were formed between bureaus of official statistics run by statisticians and economists of high caliber, and an academic world itself mobilized by the

administration's demands for expertise. This period witnessed the development not only of quantitative sociology based on sampling surveys, in Chicago or at Columbia, but also of national accounts on which, between the 1940s and the 1970s, policies inspired by Keynesianism were later based.[48]

The increasing prominence of the role of the state in organizing intellectual life in the United States saw its counterpart in the parallel political and intellectual reorganization of the rest of the world. As Timothy Mitchell has observed,

> only in the interwar period did official and academic knowledge begin to picture the world as a series of nation-states. With the growing strength of anti-imperialist movements in the colonial world, the collapsing of European empires, and the development by the United States of more effective forms of imperialism—in Central America and the Caribbean, the Pacific, and the Persian Gulf—based upon nominally sovereign local regimes, the globe came to be seen no longer as a network of empires but as a system of presumptively equivalent nation-states.[49]

Earlier work based on the "color line" of W.E.B. Dubois and others vanished, superseded by the territorial state, which was both a precursor to and competitor of the interdisciplinary area studies initiatives of the postwar period. But again, we get ahead of ourselves.

Whatever residual reluctance to collaborate with the government that university-based social scientists continued to exhibit during the Depression was entirely extinguished by the outbreak of World War II. Indeed, in the United States, the disinterested stance of "pure research" was associated with German university traditions and attributed some responsibility for the rise of

Nazism.[50] The intimate relations of American social scientists and government policymakers in the New Deal and during World War II suspended the mediated relationship that had developed with the expansion of the research universities in the first decades of the century and reflected the sense of emergency entailed by the Depression and war. It helped that these emergencies created "demand for purely operational, applied scholarship in the service of relatively uncontested policy goals."[51] Even liberals skeptical about the merits of the welfare state could hardly fault the pursuit of social and scientific knowledge in support of peace and prosperity—or, at least, to end war and poverty.

After the remarkable of achievements of the government-backed, university-based Manhattan Project, which culminated in construction of the first atomic weapon, basic scientific research, particularly physics, enjoyed a sort of glamour in the academy and beyond that it had never before possessed. Basic science soon surpassed engineering as the realm most deserving popular support, and the National Science Foundation was established to ensure continued government funding of research in the sciences. Engineering and the applied sciences took a back seat to basic scientific research as the model for—and presumed engine of—scientific and technological development until the 1980s, when engineering saw a resurgence in the computer revolution. Social science was not included in the NSF's original mandate, in part because the distinction between basic and applied research—asking questions and seeking answers—was less unambiguous, although the establishment of the White House's Council of Economic Advisors in 1946 symbolized the deference the government seemed prepared to pay to social science.

Nonetheless, the end of World War II and with it what Ira Katznelson has called the "demobilization of federal social science" released hundreds of social scientists with varied and significant experience in government back into American universities. At the same time, private foundations resumed support of social sciences, emphasizing support for university-based research. In the ten years between 1948 and 1958, foundation support for academic social science reached more than $85 million, almost half of which went to Berkeley, Columbia, and Harvard. In the next five years, the Ford, Rockefeller, and Carnegie Foundations gave nearly $100 million to political science departments, half of which went to those same three institutions alone.[52]

Although the return of the social scientists to the universities and the revival of foundation funding reaffirmed American liberalism's preference for the private sector, these social scientists believed their science had served a good cause and they intended that their university careers would continue to reflect a commitment to the public good through scientific advance. Lasswell's impotent social scientists seemed a distant nightmare as this generation shaped America's universities as research environments "independent of the state but supportive of the regime."[53] They were helped in that by the growth of government funding of higher education and scientific research. Unlike that of the private foundations, postwar federal funding was not principally directed to the social sciences but it had an enormous impact on the professional lives of American social scientists nonetheless; between 1940 and 1990, federal funds for higher education increased by a factor of twenty-five, enrollment by ten, and average teaching loads were reduced by half. [54] In 1945, 15 percent of all Americans had attended college; by the end of the twentieth century, half of all adult American had spent time in college (in contrast to under 15 percent in the United Kingdom). During the second half of the twentieth century the number of colleges and universities in the United States more than doubled, from 1,800 to 4,000.[55] Postwar optimism, in the 1950s as in the 1920s, made an intimate partnership between social science and government seem both desirable and feasible. Indeed, in the U.S., Harold Lasswell himself expressed the optimism of the era in his advocacy of a new discipline, which he called "policy science."

The 1960s thus began with high hopes and unprecedented opportunities for social scientists to test their theories and methods on important and challenging problems, from the domestic issues of racism, poverty, and urban blight to the international challenge of containing communism. John Kennedy's recruitment of high-powered academic social scientists into his policy circles and Lyndon Johnson's embrace of the interventionist state in programs associated with his Great Society seemed to bode well for scientific, rational public policy.[56] It was not long, of course, before disillusionment set in as an entire generation of university students challenged the model of social engineering which had shaped the relationship between social science and public policy for decades.

In his last address as President, Dwight D. Eisenhower warned that, like the relationship he famously described as "the military-industrial complex," the links between government and universities were also fraught with danger. Eisenhower, who had served as president of Columbia University before his election as President of the United States, cautioned that "the prospect of the domination of the nation's scholars by Federal employment, project allocations, and the power of money is ever present—and is gravely to be regarded."[57] It was a view that would become increasingly widespread.

As problems in both domestic and foreign policy proved less tractable than expected, social scientists grew dismayed by the limitations of their influence. Perhaps drawing too heavily on their experience of the wartime mobilization, when an undeclared but very real state of emergency had suspended ordinary politics and created an exceptional consensus, they expected that social science expertise would easily and instantly be translated into policy. As Leslie Pal observed, "a decision-making process which refused to apply [their] knowledge when it was offered was, almost by definition, perverse and quixotic,"[58] and it was certainly frustrating to the social scientists themselves.

As the upheavals of the 1960s gained strength, however, it was apparent that both the students and the general public were less concerned about the limitations on the use of technocratic expertise in policymaking than about the absence of such limitations. Criticism came from all quarters: Alabama governor George Wallace's segregationist attacks on the federal government included condemnations of "pointy-headed professors" while social scientists, particularly those who retained close ties with the government, were conspicuous targets of student rage on university campuses. What had once seemed to be a virtuous if somewhat arrogant involvement in public service was transmuted virtually overnight into a naive collaboration with an immoral regime.[59] The optimism and excitement of the 1950s came to look like overconfidence and self-absorption, as the radical critics of the 1960s implicated social scientists in policies that they characterized as both technically maladroit and morally bankrupt.

THE RETREAT OF THE SOCIAL SCIENCES AND THE ESTABLISHMENT OF POLICY SCHOOLS

The social science community's reaction to this disheartening experience was to retreat into the university and their disciplines. One-time consultants at the university repudiated government contracts, leaving the government to rely on a small band of loyalists, largely from outside the university and rarely with the highest standing in the disciplines. Controversy erupted in 1965 around Project Camelot, a U.S. Department of the Army effort to enlist social scientists in developing "social conflict theory" which would contribute to the Army's efforts to "counter insurgencies" in developing countries, particularly in Latin America. Provoking widespread condemnation throughout Latin America itself, opposition to Project Camelot represented one of the first international collaborations among social scientists. As Johann Galtung, a Norwegian sociologist educated at Columbia University, whose inquiries sparked the debate, observed at the time that "there have probably been few issues that have united empiricists, phenomenologists, and Marxists alike as effectively." The project was canceled, but not before a major debate about the propriety of scholarly collaboration in U.S.-government-sponsored projects had been launched.[60]

By 1975, the "policy science" movement was spent—and Paul Lazarsfeld wrote its obituary when he observed that he could never figure out what it was[61]—and many social scientists abandoned active participation in public policy to focus instead on development of their disciplines as ends in themselves. "Embarrassed by moralism or sentiment," university social scientists repudiated any claims to public service and rested their claims to authority on narrow interpretations of their scientific expertise.[62] Perhaps ironically, the growth of federal research support, about which many were now ambivalent, had already laid the groundwork for an inward focus on the disciplines on the part of social scientists.

In part this reflected generational change. As Weintraub points out, those who had elected careers as economists in the

1930s were "impelled to study economics by the great social dislocations of the time, the Great Depression and the battle over ideologies—socialism, individualism." Students who trained in PhD programs in the 1950s and 1960s were seduced by the romance, and the federal funding, of post–World War II and especially post-Sputnik science: "Economics by the 1960s had become a science of building, calibrating, tuning, testing and utilizing models constructed out of mathematical and statistical econometric materials."[63]

While the policy of peer review, enshrined in National Science Foundation, Department of Education and other government proposal review processes, guaranteed academic freedom and discouraged personal or political bias, it also fostered a self-referential focus on the estimates of professional colleagues at the expense of attention to problems of society at large and it reinforced already calcified disciplinary boundaries. This retreat was made possible, and its consequences shaped, by the nature of the U.S. employment market. Unlike the German university system, for example, where the relatively small number of full professorships required that the incumbents cover their fields broadly, in the United States, professorial positions proliferated in the 1960s, both within growing universities and as a function of the increasing numbers of institutions of higher education. This growth permitted greater specialization and weakened the dominance of intellectual fields by one or two schools.[64] The prewar heyday of Columbia's anthropology department under Franz Boas, Margaret Mead, Ruth Benedict, and their colleagues, or its sociology department in the 1940s and 1950s under Paul Lazarsfeld and Robert Merton, reflected not only the intellectual power of these field leaders but also the concentration of social science research in a relatively small number of institutions. Larger numbers in the postwar period created more specialization, more competition, and less discipline-wide intellectual coherence, not to say policy utility.

The desire to address the problems of society at large, and the liberal moralism and sentiment so often attached to it, did not disappear in the absence of attention from the social sciences. Instead they found perhaps surprisingly congenial receptions at the university in the humanistic disciplines. From the outset, of course, the social sciences were projects of the national elite and American social scientists had found reassurance in their association with power. Ironically, given their origins in liberalism's moral improvement, their ambivalence about where to rest their claims to authority and the historical identification of social science with the power elite meant that social scientists were relatively ill-equipped to recognize and respond to the expansion of political participation and civic engagement marked by the 1960s. It proved to be departments of English, history, and anthropology that best accommodated the demands for change in society and at the university, as they "assumed a new social function: to study and fortify the culture of the previously excluded."[65]

The withdrawal of the social scientists from active engagement, the growing willingness of humanistic disciplines to embrace social issues, and the demise of policy science left those concerned about the conduct of public policy in a quandary. The upheavals of the 1960s, from civil rights to Vietnam, and the 1970s, from Watergate to stagflation, provided ample evidence that there was room for improvement in public policy and public administration in the United States. The humanists had adopted a distant, ironic, and critical posture entirely, if not always deliberately, consistent with liberalism's skepticism; as Edward Said, an exemplar of moral engagement anchored in the humanities, put it, "the intellectual, as opposed to the professional, is someone who is, by the very virtue of this vocation, an opponent of consensus and orthodoxy."[66]

While celebrating and protecting their role as home of the social critic, American research universities had little outlet for the vague sense of moral obligation that continued to infuse—and justify—their mission. The study of public administration itself, once a thriving field within political science, was represented in state-supported institutions but rarely in major research universities, for it had lost touch with the theoretical and methodological developments in the social sciences. As Werner Jann observed, "instead of being an innovator, [public administration] became a 'slightly out-of-date purveyor of almost-current practice.' "[67]

The time was ripe for yet another effort to reconcile the social ←— sciences and public policy, before social science lost touch with its research domain in pursuit of self-regarding theoretical and methodological development and public policy was relegated to an equally self-referential pursuit of best practices. Once again, it was the private foundations which shaped this effort, as the Ford Foundation stepped in to support the establishment of a new generation of professional graduate schools of public policy in the 1970s. From the Haas School of Public Policy at Berkeley to the Kennedy School of Government at Harvard (and ultimately, the MPA program at Columbia's School of International and Public Affairs), these new schools and programs were designed to respond to the dilemmas posed for both social science and government by the developments of the 1960s and 1970s. The social scientists needed data, informants, audiences, and research challenges from what was by then known as "the real world." The welfare state needed staff who could use new social scientific tools and methods, including large data sets and mathematical models.

These schools were to serve as a conduit between the social science research of the academy and the world of public affairs.[68]

The public policy curriculum quickly became quite stylized. The new initiative was assertively interdisciplinary although economics and sociology were better represented than political science. Policymakers were no longer expected to be carried away by the elegance and simplicity of the solutions proposed by social scientists, however, and it was widely acknowledged that the political environment of policy was something policymakers and administrators needed to understand.[69] As Jann astutely observed, the curriculum devised to serve this purpose exhibits a normative commitment that is no less powerful for being almost invisible to its adherents. As he put it, there

> developed a division of labor in which microeconomics deals with what *should* be done while political and organizational analysis is used to find out what *can* be done. . . . Political analysis is only concerned with tactical questions of how to implement what economics tells us we should do. Could it not also be the other way around? . . . politics is seen only as something that disturbs rational policy making.[70]

For the next several decades, these schools of public policy would live in uneasy proximity to the social sciences within their universities, often viewed as unsatisfying compromises, scientifically less rigorous than the social sciences and morally less engaged than the humanities. Indeed, in some ways, the policy schools mirrored the relationship that had developed earlier between the discipline of economics and the business schools, which added "management science" to "applied economics" and thereby permitted the academic economists to ignore applied science and indulge their tastes for very formal and mathematically complex theoretical work. In some respects, the existence of policy schools produced the same reaction among political scientists, institutionalizing and perhaps exacerbating the tension between the discipline and the "applied science" of public policy.[71]

By the beginning of the twenty-first century, public policy schools were beginning to reflect on the implications of their curricular biases. As Martin Lipsky, former staffer to the Governor of Massachusetts and lecturer at Harvard's Kennedy School observed,

> Institutionally, the Kennedy School rests on the idea of speaking truth to power. The practical consequence of that is to devalue politics. Students get the message that their role is to squeeze the role of politics out of policy-making, that politics is a dirty business, that politics gets in the way of good government. That's not the way the real governmental world exists.[72]

Ultimately, social scientists like James Scott would criticize the very project of state policy informed by social science, outlining "the logic behind the failure of some of the great utopian social engineering schemes of the twentieth century."[73]

Disciplinary loyalties were impressed upon apprentice social scientists during their graduate training, but by the end of the twentieth century and thanks in part to the expansion of social science research itself in new departments and new universities, the disciplines were as much artifacts of university departmental organization as they were genuine research traditions. Their members often displayed a jealousy of their territory and a readiness to disparage their rivals if they thought it would secure them university resources, but much of the disciplinary chauvinism had the flavor of bravado. For all of the highly ritualized and stylized processes and procedures for review, very few social scientists could be confident that their research was prized by society, that their students would be sought after, their articles circulated, their ideas borrowed and built upon, or ultimately that their societies would any better for their work[74] Under these circumstances, the temptations of petty disciplinary pride and jealousy were hard to resist.

Certainly, social scientists who were developing new methods and approaches betrayed a satisfaction in their work that transcended disciplinary prejudice. The common purpose in methodological innovation and theoretical development—in what prove to be dead ends as well as in genuine advances—infected disciplines with little regard to their formal boundaries. Cultural studies enticed anthropologists, historians, geographers; game theory intrigued economists, sociologists, psychologists; political scientists seemed ready to jump on both bandwagons. New advances in quantitative methods and statistical techniques were shared across all the social sciences.

In much of the social sciences, however, the power of the economist's model of human behavior was contested even as it seemed triumphant, reflected in the flourishing of formal, rational approaches to theory and method. The alternatives represented in institutionalist and constructivist perspectives linked the core social sciences with the guest disciplines of history and anthropology, as well as with the humanities. Reflecting many of the same controversies that constituted the labor pains of modern economics at the turn of the preceding century, this debate was not only—or even principally—a question of method. As Craig Calhoun has observed, it counterpoises two views of the origins of the public good, contrasting those who believe that the public good is to be found, existing in nature to be discovered and cultivated, with those who believe it is forged or constructed at particular historical moments and geographical places.[75] Obviously, the implications of these profoundly divergent perspectives for the making of public policy are enormous, representing as they do conflicting definitions of liberalism as well as of science, but they were not questions either the public policy practitioners or the social scientists of the day were prepared to take up.

Indeed, the very growth of American political and economic power in the world, and concomitant increasing U.S. influence in shaping social science and public policy research seemed to permit a complacency about the sources and purposes of social science insight. As Whitley suggests, the "American model" was being adapted everywhere:

> internationalized' sciences . . . reflect the dominant characteristics of the most important national system in the field. . . . Increasingly, research skills and strategies have become determined by the pattern of education and employment characteristic of the United States.[76]

Yet, just at this apparent moment of triumph, the ground upon which the relationship between social science and public policy was built in the United States had begun to shift. American liberalism's skepticism about the state revived, fueled in part by the same disappointment in the welfare state that had led to the creation of that new generation of public policy schools, and American influence in the world meant that this perspective was quickly taken up around the world. The revolutions of Reagan, Thatcher, and Gorbachev, and the emergence of the aptly named "Washington consensus" in development circles, all converged on a normative model which distrusts the state and the logic of politics and relies on the market to serve the public good.

By the end of the twentieth century, the methods and ideas—the knowledge—created by the social sciences permeated everyday life, as we will see, certainly in the United States, and increasingly elsewhere. Neither the state nor the university any longer enjoyed a monopoly on social science research, nor for that matter on public service. The centuries-long process by which the state absorbed authority and the decades-long history of university collaboration in the specifically liberal history of that process in America was spent. New models of public policy and new sites of social science research were appearing, and it seemed unlikely that the institutions that had shaped and supported the scientific and policy communities for the preceding century would emerge unchanged.

3

A Marketplace of Ideas

*Social Science and Public Policy
Beyond Government*

As we saw in the last chapter, the systematic pursuit of social inquiry was initially prompted by the development of the modern
state in Europe, but as it developed in the United States during
the nineteenth century, the incarnation of that element of the relationship between all modern states and their societies was profoundly shaped by American liberalism. The social sciences we
know today were themselves an inventive marriage of the scientific temperament of the time with the mission of moral improvement that marked American liberal ideology, and from the
outset, they exhibited an abiding affinity with liberalism in their
questioning of authority, claims to universalism, celebration of
the individual, and reliance on freedom of belief and association.
American liberalism's skepticism about (not to say hostility toward) the state, and its celebration of private initiative on behalf
of the public good, encouraged sponsorship of social research
on behalf of, but outside, the public sector. The rapid rise of the
research university in the late nineteenth century provided a site

for research that was at once dispassionate about the partisan politics of the day and profoundly committed to the liberal ideological foundations of the American state.

By the 1920s, the partnership between the major research universities and the large private foundations that were another unique invention of American liberal capitalism reinforced the marriage of the impulse to social improvement with a research venue thought to be uncontaminated by either an overbearing state or what Americans would come to call "the special interests" of the private sector. Thus, for much of the twentieth century, American social scientists occupied a very special position. Generously supported in their research endeavors, they could maintain a decorous distance from the compromising fray of both politics and the market, content in what seemed to be disinterested service of social progress through science. They viewed themselves as members of an elite, a meritocracy with knowledge and skills that made them important participants in national life.

Because of the scientific indeterminacy and normative essence of social research, however, social scientists often exhibited a measure of anxiety about their status and influence. From the 1930s to the 1960s, this concern was alleviated by participation in the great projects of constructing the welfare state at home and projecting American power abroad. The popular revolts of the 1960s against both domestic and foreign policy in the United States revealed the contradictions in this effort to reconcile the aspirations to both scientific standing and policy influence, and social scientists withdrew from their association with public policy and turned instead to building self-reinforcing communities of scientific professionals organized around the disciplines that had emerged seventy-five years earlier.

This withdrawal from public engagement not only left those concerned with social improvement and public policy at a loss for expert advice, it also failed to assuage the unease that social scientists had exhibited about their place and purpose in the world virtually since the beginning of the social sciences themselves. Because the social sciences could ride the coattails of expanding American political and economic power throughout the world during the latter decades of the twentieth century, some of that anxiety was alleviated by the appearance of authority, thanks to growing nongovernmental and international audiences for social science. Yet these new audiences brought profound challenges to the practice of both social science and public policy.

MARKET VS. STATE AS THE ENGINE OF PUBLIC POLICY

These developments were taking place in the context of profound transformations in the very nature of the societies about which social scientists claimed expertise. The upheavals of the 1960s marked the end of the expansion of the welfare state in the United States and, as it turned out, throughout the world. By the dawn of the twenty-first century, American liberal ideology seemed triumphant at home and abroad, producing the retreat of the state or, perhaps better, the expansion and diffusion of sites aspiring to influence public policy, in what might be called marketization of public policy. Certainly, much of the talk about the capacity of the market to allocate values more efficiently than the state or about the ability of civil society to represent an engaged and organized citizenry more effectively than the state was just that—talk. But when Ronald Reagan, Margaret Thatcher, and Mikhail Gorbachev all said it at the same time it became, for at least a while, public policy. Causes for everything from the collapse of communism to the failure of economic development were found in overweening state interference in the what were said to be the natural workings of the market.

Whether or not this diagnosis was accurate, the world-wide prescription was the same: the state should recede in favor of economic and social actors. In the Soviet Union, restructuring—*perestroika*—was embraced as the solution to the problems of communism, and ultimately, of course, produced its demise. The first President George Bush followed Ronald Reagan's celebration of "the magic of the marketplace" by commending voluntary engagement with his vision of a "thousand points of light" illuminating American society. The International Monetary Fund and World Bank's expression of what became known as the Washington Consensus was perhaps less rhetorically extravagant but the message was the same; the Bank's report on the Middle East, for example, scolded that "for too long, countries in the Middle East and North Africa (MENA) region have squandered their potential. . . . The huge investments in state-owned enterprises and human skills unsuited to today's marketplace are the nub of the adjustment problem facing most MENA countries."[1]

Around the world, people listened—and for good reason. Market capitalization of many major corporations was beginning to exceed the GDP of most countries: at the end of 1999, for example, at $155 million, Home Depot was about the same size as Bangladesh, at $161 billion, Merck equaled Ukraine, and at $296 billion, Wal-Mart approached the size of Argentina.[2] Developing countries repositioned themselves as emerging markets and looked to foreign direct investment to finance economic transformation; in 1990, UNDP created a Division for Private Sector Development, and the United Nations itself began to reexamine its own operations with an eye to making them more efficient and business-friendly. In 1990, private firms invested a little over $43 billion in the developing world; in 1997, the number had risen to $252 billion, compared to $77 billion from the World Bank and other public sector sources.[3] Soon, with competition for markets getting fiercer, large transnational corporations were using what was known as "corporate social responsibility"—financing development projects, respecting human rights, protecting the environment—as a vehicle to win business. This trend culminated in the announcement in 1999 of the Global Compact, a "initiative to unite the UN and business in a joint effort to safeguard open markets . . . "[4]

The urge to privatize went even to the core responsibilities of the state; as P. W. Singer pointed out, private military firms (PMFs) were proliferating, and "the emergence of the PMFs challenges one of the basic premises of international security: that states possess a monopoly over the use of force." At the beginning of the twenty-first century, large business firms worked for virtually every military establishment in the world, providing everything from communications and information technology support for the United States' military arsenal to air defense and naval training for Saudi Arabia, and they played important roles in virtually all of the post–Cold War conflicts, from Croatia to Angola. Much of the personnel of the PMFs was drawn from military units declared surplus after the Cold War, particularly in Russia, or after the demise of repressive regimes, as in South Africa.[5]

The private sector was not the only beneficiary of the lowered ambitions of the state. Not-for-profit and nongovernmental organizations (NGOs) flourished, providing both service delivery and policy research and advocacy. In the United States, for example, the nonprofit sector had actually begun to grow well before Presidents Reagan and Bush commended it to their citizens: in 1953, there were 50,000 charitable tax-exempt organizations registered with IRS; by the mid-1980s they had reached nearly a million. Many arenas of fundamental public interest were largely in the hands of the nonprofit sector: in 1990, nonprofit hospitals provided two-thirds of the patient days of hospital care, and non-profit childcare facilities accounted for 56 percent of the children in daycare. All told, nonprofits accounted for 15 percent of total employment in the United States in the early 1990s, and this trend was apparent around the world, as nonprofit employment in a number of European countries met or exceeded the American figures.[6]

In public policy research and advocacy, the proliferation of think tanks with active partisan agendas accelerated in the 1970s. The first generation—the Council on Foreign Relations, the National Bureau of Economic Research, the Brookings Institution, all founded in the 1920s—shared a vaguely liberal, internationalist, and progressive commitment to American power, international peace, and domestic welfare. After the Second World War, a generation of think tanks quite closely associated with the government—and quite reliant on government contracts—including the RAND Corporation, for example, and the Hudson Institute—appeared and they too supported the American regime. Their focus was generic public policy and, like their predecessors, they claimed a nonpartisan policy posture. In the 1960s and 1970s, a new generation of think tanks began to appear; these were both more narrowly focused on particular policy domains—the environment, for example, or urban policy—and more willing to take an explicitly partisan stance—very often quite critical of the government. The Washington-based Institute for Policy Studies was a vocal critic of American policy in Vietnam in the 1960s and, while some of the bastions of the New Right were actually fairly old—the American Enterprise Institute had been established in 1943—they grew more vocal and more influential as they were joined in the 1970s by like-minded groups. Of all the think tanks in the U.S., more than half had been established since the 1970s and, by the standards of their predecessors, most of these were "increasingly entrepreneurial, and more likely to be specialized, more directly policy focused and partisan in their research and analysis."[7]

In the aftermath of the September 11 attacks, for example, the Washington Institute for Near East Policy (WINEP) placed nearly ninety articles and opinion pieces written by its members in major newspapers in the United States, the United Kingdom, and Israel; by contrast, university-based experts on the Middle East expressed frustration at the difficulties they encountered in finding public exposure for their analysis. "The expertise on the Middle East that exists in universities is not being utilized, even for basic information," worried Juan Cole, professor of history at the University of Michigan and editor of the field's most prestigious outlet, the *International Journal of Middle East Studies.* At least part of the disparity was attributable to the fact that although the staff at WINEP and similar organizations carried "university-style titles such as 'senior fellow' and 'adjunct scholar' . . . their research is very different from that of universities— it is entirely directed towards shaping government policy."[8]

As David Featherman, former President of the Social Science Research Council, and his colleagues observed, "It is perhaps ironic that academics in disciplines such as economics, political science, and sociology—in their quest for professional integrity and scientific objectivity—may have unintentionally undermined these disciplines' long term relevance to policy and thereby conceded the main battlefield to the private, often partisan, think tanks."[9]

Around the world, such think tanks and policy advocacy organizations were also proliferating and by the beginning of the twenty-first century, there were estimated to be at least 3,000, operating "in almost every country that has more than a few million people and a modicum of intellectual freedom."[10] In the developing countries and transition economies, the traditions of university-based social science research were weak, reflecting in part the weakness of the states that would have been early consumers of social science. As we shall see, much of the social science activity was conducted by international researchers, trained in American and European universities, according to American and European standards. In the Third World, the traditional role of the NGO community reflected the incapacity of the state, as NGOs played a considerable role in service provision, international humanitarian assistance, and development. But equally critical has been the growing advocacy role played by NGOs in support of human rights, the environment, and improving the status of women and children.[11] Only twenty years after it was founded, Human Rights Watch, for example, was an influential voice not merely in monitoring and advocacy around the world but also in debates about the shape of international institutions such as the International Criminal Court. The awarding of the Nobel Peace Prize to the Campaign to Ban Landmines in 1998 attested to the increasingly significant role of NGOs in international politics.

In American schools of public policy, administrators routinely bemoaned the declining interest of their students in jobs in the public sector. As Primack observed,

> The idea that public service should come in many sizes and shapes has taken hold in communities across the nation. But at the same time that public service has taken hold of the national imagination in new forms, the old fashioned concept of service in government has suffered. . . . Even in graduate and profes-

sional schools of public policy, the number of students seeking to take government jobs has steadily declined in recent years.[12]

Primack attributed this trend to several factors—low government salaries and high student debt, uncompetitive recruiting practices in the public sector and, tellingly, the increasingly common practice of government outsourcing, which created public policy opportunities in not-for-profit organizations and private consulting firms.

In fact, even higher education itself was being reshaped by marketization. At the end of the century, there were an estimated 100 million students in post-secondary education around the world, and increasing numbers of them were in private schools, including a growing number of private, for-profit schools. More than three quarters of the students in South Korea, Japan, the Philippines, and Taiwan studied in private universities; by contrast, just 20 percent of American university students, and an even smaller fraction of Europeans, were at private schools. While some of the world's best universities were private, and most countries regulated private university-level education, some of the new schools were little more than diploma mills, meeting a demand, if not for education, certainly for credentials which would enhance the job prospects and life chances of their bearers.[13]

The international marketplace for higher education was creating incentives for reform throughout the world—even in its birthplace, Europe. After UNESCO reported that the vast majority of the world's non-European international students chose to attend universities in the United States, Australia, and Canada, the education ministers of thirty-two European countries convened in Prague to implement the "European Higher Education Area" announced in 1999 in Bologna. Comparable degrees and degree titles and requirements were to enhance the comprehensibility and desirability of European advanced education. More and more European universities were offering courses, even whole degrees, in English. Bernd Waechter, director of the Brussels-based Academic Cooperation Association, opined that "it's a welcome development that governments all over Europe have woken up to the new economic realities."[14]

THE DEMOCRATIZATION
OF SOCIAL SCIENCE

The growth in the variety of sites that delivered public services and conducted public policy research accompanied and fostered the democratization of the social sciences. Far from the exclusive meritocracy it had been as late as the 1960s, the world of the social sciences broadened and deepened dramatically. Indeed, by the turn of the century, the social sciences shaped the methods and approaches of policymakers nearly everywhere around the world, while annual governmental expenditures worldwide for the collection of the social and economic data that are the building blocks of social science research reached billions of dollars.[15]

The association of social science with the university in the United States also created an audience of nonspecialist consumers there, and social science ideas, approaches and methods seeped into ordinary discourse.[16] By the end of the century a quarter of adult Americans had a college degree[17] and, while we must assume that not all of those graduates were social science majors, much of the language of modern social life reflected their exposure to the methods and the findings of social science. As Pal puts it,

Social Science influences public policy in the same way that water seeps through limestone . . . think of the various ways a social scientist distributes ideas and research: specialized articles and books, routine undergraduate and graduate teaching, conferences, colloquia, public speeches, committee appearances, commissioned and contract work, newspaper and magazine writing, radio and TV commentary . . . who knows by what strange alchemy one's ideas might effect public policy? Decision-makers, in short, pick up social scientific ideas many ways, not least by many of them having been students of social scientists while attending university.[18]

From program evaluation to cost-benefit analysis, environmental impact reporting to macroeconomic forecasting and public opinion polling, American newspapers were full of the language of social science, and their editors evidently expected that their readers would understand and appreciate this analytical perspective.

Indeed, for most Americans, and for many other people in the world, the social scientific conception of knowledge was very familiar. They lived in a world that valued quantification, measured reality in numerically precise, probabilistic terms, and favored, if not required, a conception of the human self as a data point, a statistic—as "human capital."[19] Even advertisers understood this: in the summer of 2000, the Bill and Melinda Gates Foundation announced its support for the Global Alliance for Vaccines and Immunization in an advertisement in *The New York Times* that illustrated both the widening familiarity with quantitative discourse and a slipping grasp on English grammar. Under a picture of several children, the caption read: "for a hopeless statistic, they look so real and lifelike."[20] Not only did

lottery ticket purchasers and stock market investors calculate—
or miscalculate—the value of their investments with elementary
probability theory but, as *The New York Times* reported shortly
before Superbowl 2000, most, but not all, major league football
coaches could calculate the expected value of a two-point con-
version attempt.[21]

This comfort with the analytical techniques of social science
was widely shared in advanced industrial countries—political
polling, mass marketing, medical research had popularized the
vocabulary of quantitative economics and statistics—so much so
that it was often forgotten that it was by no means universal. Yet
even in the United States, resistance to being a "nameless, face-
less number" was the stuff of late-twentieth-century American
folklore, and, as popular reactions to reports of leaking nuclear
waste or news of miracle cancer cures suggested, skepticism
about "lies, damn lies, and statistics" does not necessarily abate
in the face of threats to personal health and well-being. Nonetheless, it is fair to say that one of the odd attributes of modernity,
and particularly American modernity, is the extent to which ordinary people become amateur social scientists, self-conscious
of themselves as data points in clinical trials, as members of the
baby boom generation, as "having demographics."[22] Social science has clearly contributed ideas, approaches, and perspectives
to public life and perforce to public policy making well beyond
the state.

The democratization and popularization of the social sciences seemed destined to reduce the intellectual cohesion of the
disciplines and increase the status anxiety of their practitioners.
As Richard Whitley suggests, for example, "the social survey
techniques which reigned over US sociology for a time" are now
widely adopted by other social scientists and policy practitioners "and so it is unclear what is the distinctive competence of so-

ciologists that requires advanced education and which enables them to deal with distinctive problems."[23] Increasing interest in "interdisciplinary" and "multidisciplinary" research illustrated both the persistence of the disciplinary templates and the growing qualms about their utility.

As social science was being democratized, the sites that claimed authority to make and implement public policy were also proliferating. New sites of education and advocacy, of public policy broadly construed, were appearing in alliances that until only recently had been almost unimaginable. Perhaps private sector support of a business training center was not that novel but the association of the United Nations Development Programme with Chevron and Citigroup in establishing just such a center in Kazakhstan suggested that new actors were engaging in both education and advocacy. UNDP's project with the Norwegian oil company, Statoil, and the human rights advocacy group Amnesty International to train Venezuelan judges on human rights issues yet again illustrated a profoundly new environment for the application of social sciences in public policy. What was the impact of the growing role of nongovernmental actors and their allies in the academy as producers and consumers of social science research? As Gagnon asks, does this pluralization and diffusion mean "merely an increase in the influence of social science [or does it] signal a more fundamental change in the relations between social science, state and society?"[24]

At the turn of the century, governments around the world were reconsidering their involvement in funding advanced research and higher education, and much research activity was moving out of universities, to privately funded, for-profit think tanks and consulting firms. Indeed, with government blessing— and often government-sponsored and financed incentives—universities themselves were turning to the private sector to sponsor their research operations, as governments increasingly argued that university-industry alliances could "create knowledge and wealth simultaneously."[25] The federal government share of all research and development spending in the United States peaked in 1964 at two-thirds; by 1995, it was down to one-third. Federal funding of academic research has remained stable at 60 percent of the total, but the rate of growth has fallen steadily for over a decade. In the meantime, corporate giving to universities rose from $850 million in 1985 to $4.25 billion less than a decade later. By the mid-1990s, in the United States, 12.5 percent, of university research was funded by industry; in Germany, the figure was nearly 10 percent.[26] This growing reliance on the private sector to support university research was a world-wide phenomenon. While American scholars worried over the fate of federal funding of university-based social science research, half the world away India's Education Secretary warned that "higher education has to be market-friendly. It can't just look to government."[27]

The changing patterns of funding of research and education were reflected in the increasingly widespread notion of social science as something marketable, with producers and consumers, buyers and sellers. The language of the market permeated discussion about the value of this "product." Arthur Lupia, a political scientist, observed in the in-house magazine of the American Political Science Association, for example, that "opinions vary" about whether "political science research [is] valuable to society." In order to, as he put it, "reduce the uncertainty," he proposed to provide information to buyers and sellers:

> As is true for all products, interactions between producers and consumers determine the value of political science research. Producers make the product. They determine its design and

the precision of its workmanship. Producers do not, however, dictate the product's value. To have value, the product must be something that consumers want or need.[28]

The existential anxiety we have seen exhibited by social scientists about the social utility of their research for nearly a century—long expressed as concern about their political power and influence—was now characterized in terms of market position and valuation. With the world-wide retrenchment of the welfare state, governments were no longer as influential as they had been, in either defining public policy or setting intellectual agendas.

Not surprisingly, one of the first indications of the significance of this shifting terrain was in graduate training. Since the 1960s, research scholars had been concerned that funding by governments—particularly, but not solely, the American government—compromised the integrity of social science research, and they debated the costs and benefits of public sector funding of research training.[29] By the end of the century, many social scientists had begun to fear comparable—possibly greater—challenges from the potential commercialization of social science. In the short run, the consequence was the ambiguity that usually results from mixed signals. In the expectation that the university market would not absorb all their graduates, social science departments increasing encourage their PhD graduates to seek what had become known as "nonacademic employment." In doing so, university-based social scientists actively encouraged the expansion of social science research in the private sector. Because they were ambivalent about this enterprise, however, the training they provided did not always serve the students or their employers well. By the early 1990s, forty percent of the annual crop of American PhDs in economics were absorbed by nonacademic employers and many of these employers reported that these new professionals were poorly equipped to conduct empirical research or to communicate their findings effectively.[30]

Universities increasingly modeled their own internal organization on the market: as Webster and Etzkowitz put it, "departments in academia are themselves being designated profit/cost centers that must not simply balance their books but seek to generate profitable income"[31] and even professional associations found themselves forced to acknowledge the significance of declining state support. The American Political Science Association is a case in point. In December 2000, *PS: Political Science and Politics*, the association's newsletter, published two task force reports, juxtaposing the dilemmas of declining membership in the political science professional association and declining funding of political science research. The Strategic Planning Committee reported that dropping library subscriptions and declining membership dues were creating financial strains.

> First, institutions (ie libraries primarily) apparently see less of value in the Association's publications relative to other choices. Second, we have been failing of late to attract to APSA membership as many of our professional progeny, the graduate students who are apprentice political scientists, as before. Third, the stagnation of individual memberships is especially troubling against the background knowledge that APSA encompasses only about half of academic political scientists and a much lower fraction of practicing political scientists nationally.[32]

Interestingly, the Association did not draw any conclusions from these "market signals" except to advocate increasing the organization's endowment, to cushion it from further drops in revenue. This conclusion was all the more remarkable in light of the controversy about the purposes of the association and its flagship journal, *The American Political Science Review*, that had erupted earlier that year in response to an anonymous broadside launched by one "Mr. Perestroika" and quickly taken up by hundreds of other political scientists in e-mail messages and letters that circulated around the country. Much of the discussion spoke to what was viewed by the critics as an overly narrow and technical conception of political science by the Association's leaders—and an unbecomingly undemocratic procedure for selecting those leaders.[33]

A task force report on Political Science at the National Science Foundation which appeared in the same issue did not see a long-term solution to either the fiscal crisis of the Association or the intellectual challenges to the discipline in government funding:

> The social sciences are not now, and may never have been, a high priority of the NSF. In many quarters of the Foundation they are seen as "soft" sciences, lacking in rigor, and often diverted from science by advocacy and reformism. . . . As for political science at the turn of the century, it is perceived at NSF as not very exciting, not on the cutting edge of the research enterprise, and in certain quarters as journalistic and reformist. While some at NSF take in stride the red flags that grants to political science projects occasionally raise on Capitol Hill, others worry that they cost the agency the approval or support of its most important constituent. Moreover, at a time when government is in diminished favor and politics seems less exiting and less salient in the life of the nation, it is harder to argue the social contributions or policy relevance of political science.[34]

The suggestions offered to make Political Science more appealing to government funders reflected the profound ambiguity in the discipline's self-definition. On the one had, they reported that a 1998 visiting committee had

> urged the NSF to "advance the cause of science in political science" by continuing to fund "methodological training programs." "By building this most basic component of political science research," they noted, "NSF has helped foster a considerable move towards making political science a real science."

Yet, the committee itself suggested that public policy questions would be more appealing than the advancement of science:

> Recent events in Seattle [at a highly contested meeting of the World Trade Organization] demonstrated the increasing public pressure for political accountability of international economic institutions such as the WTO. Might we not press NSF to recognize, by new program or interdisciplinary initiative, such a vital and lively topic and its related scholarship?[35]

After the terrorist attacks of September 11, 2001 the picture seemed to brighten slightly. John Marburger, Director of the White House Office of Science and Technology Policy, remarked in a talk delivered the following April that "the social sciences in general have much more to offer on the difficult problems of our time than we are currently acknowledging." Marburger, a physicist, speculated that the failure of policymakers to avail themselves of social science research was because "the social sciences suffer from treating issues that are so familiar as to breed contempt" and he acknowledged that " we are not yet systematically including the social sciences in the mobilization for the war against terrorism."[36]

Few social scientists were banking on Marburger's hopes, and it was to another distinctly American device that the political scientists turned to insulate their association from the need to respond to the "market" signals which were suggesting its failure to meet consumer demand: the association was classified as a tax-exempt charity. As a result of tax-deductible gifts, it enjoyed an endowment whose income was reported to have grown briskly and to have "provided the Association a cushion against temporary fiscal tightness."[37] And, perhaps, declining relevance.

Obviously, these trends—declining academic employment, decreasing government funding, dropping membership in professional associations—reflected the changing configuration of funding of social science research. On the "push" or what we might call the "supply" side, the long-term instability of external funding, subject as it was to large-scale changes in the roles of government and business and the new and as yet volatile relationship of universities with the private sector, contributed to the growing importance of nontraditional sites in both the not-for-profit and private sectors in the conduct of social science research. Of growing significance, however, was the "pull" or "demand" created by the proliferation of "knowledge-based industries." These industries—from political advocacy to international communication—were producing new and newly empowered organizations which drew on the fruits of social science research to develop their positions and expand their markets. Many of the major American media outlets developed significant survey research capabilities, while labor unions created in-house research labs to administer surveys and assess public opinion. International consulting companies and accounting firms were early adopters of social science research techniques, and put them to use in monitoring labor and environmental compliance around the world. Advocacy groups, like Amnesty International and Human Rights Watch, were increasingly supplementing the fact-finding methodologies of legal investigative traditions with social scientific approaches to data collection and analysis in exposing systematic or widespread human rights abuses.

What did it mean that research conventionally understood as social science—using the same methods and approaches and often, if not always, meeting the same standards of rigor and review—was being done not only in universities but also at international accounting firms like Price Waterhouse and NGOs like Human Rights Watch? How did it change the vocation of social science and the practice of public policy? Whitley suggests that,

> Relative to the early post-war period, the influence of non-scientists on problem selection and prioritization has grown. So too has the significance of mission-oriented research funding, the variety of funding agencies and the criteria they use to select and evaluate research projects. The expansion of state funding for long-term political and social goals, such as health care improvement, in both state and university laboratories, together with the growth of non-profit and business funding of academic research, have generated both a greater pluralism of intellectual goals and more variety in the standards used to judge research excellence in the public sciences.[38]

We may start consideration of how this changing environment will shape the work and the world of the social scientist with Robert Merton's observation, more than fifty years ago, that "four sets of institutional imperatives—universalism, communism, disinterestedness, organized scepticism—comprise the ethos of modern science."[39] Each of these is implicated in the changing role of the state in mediating the relationship between social science and public policy.

PROPERTY AND THE "END OF COMMUNISM" IN SOCIAL SCIENCE

Perhaps the most startling of his imperatives, particularly at the time, was Merton's assertion of the "communism" of science. "The substantive findings of science," he wrote, "are a product of social collaboration and are assigned to the community. . . . Property rights in science are whittled down to a bare minimum by the rationale of the scientific ethic. . . . Secrecy is the antithesis of this norm."[40] Social collaboration and the public and replicable research associated with it played several significant roles in scientific development. Perhaps least obviously, but not unimportantly, they served to standardize, formalize, and reproduce the definition of scientific data. Because local knowledge is, as Scott points out, "dispersed and relatively autonomous, [it] is all but unappropriable."[41] Scientific knowledge, by contrast, creates comparable facts, and sets of facts, which are organizable and assignable.

Open collaborative research traditions also provide an effective mechanism for maintaining common methodological standards and insuring accuracy. Peer review of research in grant proposals and journal articles was an extension of the self-government of the American university, in which through its very stylized hiring and promotion procedures, the professoriate reviewed, reproduced, and renewed itself. Peer review of research served as a formalized process for the certification of research as meeting common standards of authenticity and accuracy: the methods were endorsed as legitimate tools and approaches and their use was sanctioned as appropriate. Very often the sharing of preliminary results also permitted or encouraged innovation by creating communities of scientists working on allied projects. Finally, peer recognition was a mechanism by which scientists established priority and ensured their status in the discipline as the originator of the idea or finding—a particularly important feature for social scientists given the profound ambiguity of the enterprise.[42] As Merton puts it, "it is only a seeming paradox that, in science, one's private property is established by giving its substance away. For in a long-standing social reality, only when scientists have published their work and made it generally accessible, preferably in the public print of articles, monographs, and books that enter the archives, does it become legitimately established as more or less securely theirs."[43]

In practice, of course, secret or proprietary research has taken place in both public and private sectors since the beginning of research itself. Indeed for American social scientists over the last half century, government classification of intelligence-related research was far more troubling than unpublished work supported by private business. As we have seen, the propriety of collaborating with government research operations, particularly those involved in foreign affairs, had long been a bone of contention among social scientists. In the 1960s, many anti-war academics joined in condemning their colleagues who worked with the U.S. government in prosecuting the wars against what were portrayed as "communist-backed insurgencies" in Latin America, the Middle East, and Africa as well, of course, as Southeast Asia. Many social scientists, especially area specialists, were sympathetic to what they construed as nationalist movements, and some of them would shortly find common cause with those in the humanities faculty who rallied to give voice to the excluded, oppressed, and otherwise disadvantaged of the world.

Although their principal complaint was born of disagreement with the purposes to which American power was being put, or at least with the methods being marshaled to accomplish those purposes, the social scientists who refused to work with the intelligence community also objected to the culture of secrecy necessarily imposed by the demands of national security. Supporters of secrecy were often skeptical about, not to say contemptuous of, the capacity of the general public to understand the complex decisions of public policy. As Dennis points out about the scientists who were involved in development of the hydrogen bomb, their "world was far from democratic. Accountability was a problem for everyone but scientists. [Theirs was an] apolitical ideal that was a pure technocracy." [44] That apolitical ideal was abhorrent to the radicals of the 1960s, who offered democracy as the solution to the failings of the regime of the technocrats. The moral commitment to social improvement which had linked social science and public policy was deployed against the very state that had first brought them together.

In the meantime, in-house research by both government agencies and private businesses proliferated over the next several decades. Paul Evans surveyed this "private research" in Canada and concluded that, although the vast bulk of this research is never published or made public, "the total dollar amount is several times greater than social science research conducted in conventional academic settings and through peer-evaluated competitions." Although, as he points out, "many professors and professional associations feel that it is outside the boundaries of legitimate scholarly work,"[45] these sectors are increasingly significant sources of employment for PhDs, and they have increasingly large impacts on public policy decisionmaking.

Whatever the dilemmas of government influence on research and research agendas during the heyday of state-sponsored science, the ultimate commitment to serve the public interest embodied in the state ensured that the goals of the sponsor at least partly overlapped with those of scientists concerned to maintain a reputation of public spirit and scientific integrity. By contrast, in private firms, argues Whitley, "reputational systems have little or no impact on what work is done, how skills are combined and managed, or how results are evaluated."[46]

The desirability of free sharing of research was complicated still further, of course, by the development of the new information technologies in the latter years of the twentieth century. The "knowledge economy," based more on ideas than on things, seemed to hold promise for society's "knowledge-producers," notably the universities and their research faculty, the long-suffering Cinderellas of industrial capitalism. When knowledge needed to be translated into tangible products before it was useful, there was little profit to be gained for the originator of the idea, since the reproduction of its tangible embodiment was both initially expensive and subject to decreasing returns to scale. Ideas, however, cost virtually nothing to reproduce once they are hatched, so the magnitude of the returns is not determined by marginal production costs but rather by ownership and use rights—by the intellectual property rights regime. By the end of the century, in the evident hope that they were, or would be, worth more if they were withheld or access were limited, research results were routinely defined as "intellectual property."[47]

In 1980, the U.S. Congress permitted universities to patent the results of the federally funded research conducted by their faculty under the Bayh-Dole Act. While this led to handsome new revenue streams for many research universities, copyright—

the usual regulatory domain for social science—did not spark the same interest until the new information technologies permitted mass distribution of courses for sale, whereupon universities quickly took up the question. In the late 1990s, the University of California sparked a significant debate by claiming ownership of the courses its faculty developed, raising concerns that books, articles, and other academic productions would fall under the same provision.[48] Soon universities around the world were debating, and promulgating, intellectual property policies. After centuries in which individual researchers disposed of their research findings—and any royalties they might have earned from disseminating those findings—as they pleased, universities throughout the world were developing intellectual property policies designed to ensure that the institution would share in the returns to knowledge production. As Peter Evans put it, "while other forms of regulation are in disrepute, this particular form of policing is now treated as one of the cornerstones of economic civilization."[49] Merton's communism of science was under siege.

INTEREST AND DISINTEREST: ADVOCACY AND SKEPTICISM IN SOCIAL SCIENCE

In its place was appearing social research that was not the property of the community nor did it exhibit Merton's skepticism and disinterest. Evert Lindquist drew our attention to "important actors who are neither policymakers nor academic researchers, but do seek to provide information relevant to policy issues." This "policy inquiry," as he called their work, consisted of publication and convocation activities as well as the generation of information.[50] These policy analysts were not oriented to the disciplines but to decisionmakers' needs, although they were often equipped with comparable intellectual, analytical, and research tools. They were not subject to the conventions that operated to maintain quality control in the university setting: notably the dissemination of research results in peer-reviewed vehicles. Whether it was classified by the government, held as proprietary by a private business, or simply posted on a web site, the quality and independence of this research was not routinely vetted by other, presumably disinterested, social scientists.

Many of the "policy inquiry" analysts and organizations were openly committed to political advocacy and, even among those which were not, the borderline between scientific knowledge and political argument became increasingly ambiguous as a result of the growing significance of those who were.[51] In 2002 the University of Denver's Institute for Public Policy Studies published a "Public Policy Resource Guide," designed to "provide an overview of major sources of policy knowledge and research." Although it included categories for think tanks, interest groups, various media outlets, and government agencies, it ignored completely the university-based policy schools and research centers. Suggesting that the university had once protected "consumers" from "misinformation," the Guide's author, Richard Caldwell, forewarns his users that today,

"Information" in public policy is rarely "objective." Indeed, virtually every think tank, interest group, or government organization seeks power and influence in the political marketplace and in the battle of ideas. This is not said to discredit any given source, but rather to assert the fact that the "policy game" is a serious one, often played for the highest of stakes. In this game, setting the agenda and controlling the dialogue are the primary ingredients of success.[52]

The expectation of "disinterested" science in the service of public policy appeared to have vanished.

In the winter of 2000, for example, a polemic erupted after a political scientist employed by the American Federation of Teachers claimed that social scientists often disseminate their findings before they are subjected to peer review in order to win government or foundation funding and influence public policy debates. The targets of his accusations, both of whom were academic social scientists, in turn accused him of having selectively criticized researchers whose positions were opposed by the teacher's union.[53] This was not entirely new of course. As Mitchell observes, in the 1970s, dependency theory was often used in debates about U.S. foreign policy toward the Third World: "Theory was a language used to authorize rival strategies and commitments in the competing intellectual politics of the field."[54] Still, the accelerating defection of social science from the loyalties imposed by reputational standards enhanced its availability for partisan purposes and exacerbated the difficulty of assessing its quality and reliability. News organizations, once contented consumers of university-based social research, became producers as well, as they sponsored polling and survey research laboratories of their own. Perhaps not surprisingly, they voiced concern about the difficulty of assessing research not subject to the conventional review standards. In the spring of 2000, *The New York Times*, for example, worried about the extent to which "misleading or bogus social science research captures the attention of a frantic public, feeding false fears, planting misguided beliefs and distorting policy. . . . Practically every week brings news reports of what social scientists have to say."[55]

The democratization and diffusion of social science had broadened exposure to the language of social science, producing audiences for social science who are neither concerned nor competent to assess its validity. Merton's skepticism and disinterestedness seemed to be going the way of his communism. Indeed, as Etzkowitz put it, "two norms of science, ie, "disinterestedness" and "communism," have at least partially displaced by an institutional imperative to translate research into economic and social use."[56]

Not all of its practitioners were prepared to concede that acknowledging political or economic utility of social science research automatically discredited it. In 2001, the Social Science Research Council, long a bastion of "disinterested" academic scholarship, announced a project to make "activist research"—research informed by "active political commitment"—a priority for field-building activities, arguing that "activist research has the potential to lead to better research outcomes: deeper and more thorough empirical knowledge of the problem at hand, as well as theoretical understanding that otherwise would be difficult to achieve."[57] True or not, this was certainly a far cry from Merton's conception of science.

UNIVERSALISM: THE PRIVATE AND THE PARTICULAR IN SOCIAL SCIENCE

And what of universalism? This may be the most interesting challenge facing the social sciences and public policy today. Discussing universalism, Merton put it this way: "truth claims, whatever the source, are to be subjected to *preestablished impersonal criteria*" and scientific careers are freely accessible to the talented. In this, he observed, "expediency and morality coincide . . . " for, as he continued, "to the extent that a society is democratic, it provides scope for the exercise of universalistic criteria in science."[58] More than half a century later, James Scott argues, quite the contrary, that the social scientist's confidence in "rational thought and scientific laws" as providing answers to empirical questions and solutions to policy problems is "deeply authoritarian." As he puts it, "if a planned social order is better than the accidental, irrational deposit of historical practice . . . only those who have the scientific knowledge to discern and create this superior order are fit to rule."[59] Perhaps it is fairest to say, with Michael Polanyi, that scientists always had dual loyalties—to the "republic of Science" and to their state; they were democrats in theory and elitists in practice. [60]

The democratic state's deployment of academic social science had resolved, or at least mediated, this tension, allowing elitists—"meritocrats"—to work for democratically elected officials, but the retreat of the state undermined this compromise. In the absence of the state as the mediator between science and policy, it appeared that the public good could be served by multiple actors with multiple purposes and perspectives, and universalism seemed to be neither necessary nor even particularly desirable in the service of the public good. The democratization of social research and the pluralization of public policy had not secured attachment to universalist values. Indeed, as Nell Painter has suggested, in the U.S., whole new fields developed in response to the failures of liberal universalist claims, notably African-American and women's studies:

> In essence, what began as a way of keeping peace on newly desegregated campuses (appeasing black students and their allies who were demonstrating to demand curricular reform) has grown into a wide-ranging interdisciplinary field that encompasses the histories and cultures of people of the African diaspora, in particular, and the meaning of race and difference in general.[61]

In international circles as well, universalist claims seemed to foster particularist responses. Scholars worried about the inequities engendered, or reinforced, not only by the private appropriation of information and knowledge but also by the increasing dominance of the United States in providing not simply "truth claims" but even the language in which they are expressed. "The increasing dominance of American English, the digital divide . . . and the commodification of information—most evident in the emergence of media empires that combine the formerly separate domains of print, broadcast and digital media—threaten to reify the 'have not' status of much of the globe."[62]

From the rise of "special interests" to the appearance of "identity politics," from the elevation of Internet English to the growing evidence of the parochialism of local research agendas, confidence that "expediency and morality coincide" seemed to be waning. Morality no longer demanded universal adherence to "preestablished impersonal criteria." Indeed, the public good seemed to be increasingly detached from such universalist values, and the importance of the particular, even sometimes the private, was magnified and associated with social improvement.

The private and the particular were represented in two quite different ways in contemporary intellectual and policy discourse about society, as celebration of identity competed with the magic of the marketplace. Thomas Bender's description of the American university at the end of the twentieth century conveyed some of this divide in academic culture.

One cluster of scholars resides in a variety of humanities disciplines (including history and anthropology). They share weak borders, openly-declared value commitments, and a historical/cultural sensibility, which produces, inevitably, a tendency towards particularism. Another group, identifying mostly with the social sciences—in mainstream economics, political science, law, sociology, and some versions of ethics—is more oriented to tight subfields (often interdisciplinary) and to methods affirmed as objective that attend little to considerations of time and place.[63]

Different as they were, both these perspectives privileged particular identities and private choices—and disciplinary loyalties—and reflected a profound doubt about the constitution and value of a universal public, particularly the public sector.

Only one of these approaches was represented in any serious way in the American public policy schools which had been established to address the dilemmas of the American welfare state. As Jann tells us,

> The dominating consensus of the schools leaves little room for critical reflection on government structures and processes. There is little conflict and competition concerning the merits and values of institutions. Instead, economic criteria and numbers seem to be used as substitutes for consensus.[64]

Yet many of the policy activists of the early twenty-first century grew out of, or drew upon, perspectives that reflected not only faith in the market but identity politics as well. Indeed, among the union activists, environmentalists, and church groups protesting the policies of the WTO and the IMF in Seattle and Washington as the new century dawned were easily as many students influenced by political engagement of literary criticism and postcolonial studies as there were social science majors.[65]

Moreover, among the activists and analysts who were equipped with the best social science techniques—the latest intellectual, analytical and methodological tools—few, if any, anchored their moral commitments in that mastery. Thanks to the profound anxiety of the social scientists about their role in projects of social and moral improvement, these analytical perspectives and methods were presented as morally neutral, as mere techniques and tools, implying no normative commitments. At the same time, the policy analysts were not expected to share the conventions of science—the expectation of replicability, the peer review, the organized skepticism—which constituted the norms of professional life.

Taught the sources of neither the standards nor the values of their professional vocation, these policy analysts summarized many of the contradictions of American liberal institutions at the beginning of the twenty-first century. American social science's simultaneous dedication to unfettered inquiry and to democratic institutions, to both the republic of science and the liberal tradition—a dual commitment Charles Lindblom describes as "inconsistent"[66]—was possible because of the unique position of the American research university outside the state, supporting the regime or, as Wendy Steiner has observed, at once "hermetically sealed from reality and centrally constitutive of it."[67]

As the state's role in defining and protecting the public good seemed to be weakening in favor of a crowded marketplace of claims, as public policy pluralized, the university's position as a privileged site of contestation appeared more difficult to maintain. Yet it was all the more crucial since, as Craig Calhoun argued,

The public good cannot be fixed in advance because it is always in a process of reconstitution. Our debates about what is good for us are always, in part, debates about whom we want to be. Whether the issue is health care, education, prison reform, or foreign aid, questions of interest are never separable from questions of identity.[68]

If the private and the particular, interest and identity, converge in public policy, the American university's dual commitment to research and education, to scientific knowledge and moral improvement, made it an essential arena for the competition and contestation without which there is no real consensus. Yet clearly the changing context of science in general and social science in particular presented challenges not only to the university but to the very definition of knowledge as well. These challenges were only reinforced by the twin of the early-twenty-first-century process of privatization: globalization.

4

Wars and Webs

Global Public Policy and International Social Science

For much of the twentieth century, American social scientists constructed a special position in society for themselves, distant from the compromising fray of both politics and the market, yet engaged in what seemed to be disinterested service of social progress through science. They participated in the great projects of constructing the welfare state at home and projecting American power abroad. The popular revolts of the 1960s against both domestic and foreign policy in the United States revealed the contradictions in this effort to reconcile aspirations to both scientific standing and policy influence. Social scientists surrendered their intimate association with public policy and turned instead to building self-referential communities of scientific professionals organized around the disciplines that had emerged seventy-five years earlier.

The withdrawal from public engagement not only left those concerned with social improvement and public policy at a loss for much expert advice, it also failed to assuage the unease that social scientists had exhibited about their place and purpose in the world virtually since the beginning of the social sciences themselves. Soon enough the retreat of the state and the marketization of public policy that marked the last several decades of the twentieth century created still more perplexing challenges for social science. On the one hand, social scientific ideas, perspectives and methods had entered the language of ordinary discourse, shaping a wide and sympathetic audience for public policy associated with social science research. On the other hand, the pluralization and privatization of sites of both public policy and social science research seemed to threaten the very foundations of social research as a scientific enterprise, particularly in its claims to collaboration, disinterestedness, and universalism. The withdrawal of the state as the mediator between science and policy encouraged the creation of property in knowledge, limited the sites available for impartiality, and magnified the importance of the private and the particular. The liberal commitment to service of a public or common good which had been at the heart of the social sciences had so faded as to be almost unrecognizable.

Unless, of course, you saw it from a distance. And more and more people did. Like pornography, globalization is hard to define but easy to see and, while there is still surprisingly little systematic research that could provide us with a theory or even analytical perspective from which to approach it, there is little doubt that, as David Held and his collaborators put it,

> globalization reflects a widespread perception that the world is rapidly being moulded into a shared social space by economic and technological forces and that developments in one region of the world can have profound consequences for the life chances of individuals or communities on the other side of the globe.[1]

From the growth of global finance to the appearance of increasingly powerful transnational advocacy organizations, from the expansion of cross-border production and distribution networks to changing patterns of human migration, from the expanding jurisdictions of international law to the widening networks of international crime, the power and relevance of the sovereign state everywhere seemed to be confronted with new and assertive legal, political, social, and economic forces. As with all other social institutions, social science and public policy were being reshaped by these same forces.

THE GLOBALIZATION OF SOCIAL SCIENCE

In fact, social science itself was being exported around the world. American social scientists had been traveling abroad to conduct research, teach, and attend symposia for decades, and after World War II, other countries began to emulate the U.S. university system and social science disciplines. In Europe, there had remained considerable resistance, even after World War II, to Americanization. At the London School of Economics, for example, postwar "politics teaching . . . was governed in a gentlemanly fashion by Professor Michael Oakeshott, who held the views that firstly there is no such thing as political education and secondly the study of politics was certainly not a science or indeed a discipline."[2] Nonetheless, the expansion of Britain's universities and national research councils in the 1960s created room, as such expansion had a century earlier in the United States, for new "modern" conceptions of social science to find departmental homes and disciplinary expression.

So, too, the era of the 1950s and 1960s, when American graduate students could find themselves the first social scientists to do research at their field site, was soon over. What Johann Galtung had described in the 1960s as "scientific colonialism"—"a process whereby the center of gravity for the acquisition of knowledge about the nation is located outside the nation itself"—was eroding even as he wrote, in the face of growing social science communities around the world.[3] Yet these communities were hardly indigenous creations: "social science debates in Europe after 1950 were strongly influenced by 'the American model,' interrupting and truncating earlier intellectual developments."[4] In Africa, post-independence governments built national universities in the 1960s and 1970s but many—"fiercely modernist"—banned the study of anthropology in a sort of nationalist refusal to be relegated to the terrain outside the here and now.[5] As Arjomand points out, "the institutionalization of sociology in the non-Western world and its 'indigenization' is a major concern in the international sociological community, a concern that goes hand-in-hand with the question of the appropriateness of a critical approach to social knowledge and to social and developmental policy"[6]

By the 1990s, virtually every country in the world boasted a national university system and the number of countries which were closed to international social science researchers had dwindled to a handful. Economic performance was widely seen as correlated with levels and quality of higher education and investment in university level was taken as a signal of intent to compete globally. Indeed, spending on social sciences in higher education was higher among the OECD countries than in the United States itself.[7] The British newspaper *The Guardian* developed a ranking of international, largely European, universities and concluded that "top US universities lead in social sciences" but, although non-English speaking countries did rather poorly, "they are sharing in the international social science journals and

. . . their contributions do have a significant international impact as judged by citation rates."[8]

The Cold War era notion that Americans, or any other nationals, studied "foreigners"—whether allies or enemies—was being superseded by the conception of social science as collaboration across borders. Webs replaced wars as the metaphor of choice for international interactions, as new research patterns, in which social scientists participated in international networks of colleagues, appeared throughout the world. Large-scale data archives promised to facilitate cross-national, cross-regional, and international comparative research: "ultimately," argued Roberta Miller, "access to the riches of distributed data archives may advance the development of a global rather than a national perspective in research on social, economic and political trends."[9]

In part this was a reflection of the profound global reach of American social science. Although the aggregate number of PhDs produced in the United States remained fairly stable in the 1970s and 1980s, the proportion of U.S. citizens declined. Americans accounted for about two-thirds of the economics doctorates in 1977, less than half of the total by 1989, and by 2000, when the U.S. government estimated that 500,000 international students were enrolled in U.S. colleges and universities, contributing $9 billion to the U.S. economy annually, a number of distinguished economics departments, including Yale, had no Americans at all among their first-year students. The United States accounted for 30 percent of all international enrollments; Britain was next with little more than half that population of foreign students.[10] American social scientists who studied democratic institutions, urban politics, labor markets, industrial organization, adolescent behavior and family policy, and myriad other issues increasingly found themselves on research teams that took them, literally or figuratively, outside the United States, often thanks to their several generations of international graduate students.

This had implications for the shape and coherence of the social sciences. As the "not-here" began to dissolve, the demands placed on social scientists to confront—not to say understand—familiar institutions in unfamiliar circumstances increased. As Whitley points out, as research terrains spread across the globe, "knowledge of the particular circumstances in which results were generated becomes important in determining their meaning and significance and so they cannot be compared and assessed in routine ways across research sites or groups."[11] It was not apparent that the parliaments of Latin America and the finance ministries of Southeast Asia were immediately and entirely comparable to their American, or even European, counterparts, nor was it clear what those differences might mean for the study of democracy or finance.

Although relatively few American social scientists seized these questions as research problems, international social scientists were beginning to examine them and, in doing so, to reintroduce the "not-now"—history—into the study of what was fast becoming a universal "here." As the sociologist Said Arjomand put it, "the appropriation of history in our generation is . . . the antidote to the two gravest dangers of the global age: presentism and pseudo-universalism. Only with the help of history can we arrive at an understanding of cultural diversity adequate for the sociological reconstruction of locality, or rather, regionality, in the cosmopolitan context of the new era." Interestingly, part of the response to the challenge of understanding the familiar in unfamiliar circumstances reflected a continuing attachment to the areas long espoused as intellectual domains by the older U.S. area studies community. Arjomand argues that "the foundation of the Arab Association of Sociology in the 1980s and the

International Association for the Study of Persian-speaking Societies in 1996, to give two examples, are premised on the utility of a sociological approach that reflects cultural, linguistic, and civilizational distinctness.[12] Yet the legacies of old area studies patterns, in which American social scientists wrote about other countries and, if they were of a generous frame of mind, thanked local informants, continued to haunt many of these research collaborations; as Fred Halliday put it, "there is nothing less international than the national prejudices of the powerful."[13]

SOCIAL SCIENCE, THE STATE, AND LIBERALISM AROUND THE WORLD

If American social scientists were still largely oblivious to the challenge presented by globalization to their research enterprise, the fact remained that American-style social science was increasingly being practiced outside its homeland. To what extent had the perspectives and prejudices of American social science shaped public policy and social research in the rest of the world? At the turn of the twenty-first century, the notion that public policy should rest on social science was widely, though not universally, accepted by national governments, and by the cosmopolitan elite of international finance and trade, international advocacy, and cooperation. Beyond that elite, the influence of social science was uneven. To an important degree, its strength depended, as it had at the outset, on the strength of the state and of liberal values.

In Western Europe, where the modern state originated, liberalism did not prevail over its several competitors until World War II, and even then traces of corporatist models of state-society relations were apparent in the organization of higher education and social research as well as the structure of the social science disciplines. In Germany, American-style social science appeared in the newly refurbished university system after World War II; in France, where the university system had developed separately from the administration-minded *grandes écoles,* social scientific policy research had been assigned to new government research institutions. Across the continent—and even in the United Kingdom as well—the postwar period saw reform of the institutions, organizations, and instruments that fostered social science and policy research.[14] Indeed, in part because of the conservatism of European universities, social science and social scientific influence in public policy grew only outside of, and in some sense opposed to, traditional academia.[15] European empirical research had been far more often based on data collected by authorities—Durkheim's use of government statistics on suicide rates is a classic example—and the American inclination to include field research and data collection as among the tools of social science arrived late in Europe.[16] No doubt partly as a result, by European standards, U.S. public policy training exhibited "a preference for data rather than theoretical understanding . . . and most recently, for management rather than analysis."[17]

If Europeans retained their taste for law and history and their preference for publicly supported data collection and research independent of the university, however, they certainly endorsed the importance of social scientifically-based public policy. As Arjun Appaduri put it,

> there are few walks of modern life, both in the West and in some other advanced industrialized societies, in which research is not a more or less explicit requirement of plausible public policy or credible argumentation, whether the matter is child abuse or global warming, punctuated equilibrium or con-

sumer debt, lung cancer or affirmative action. Research-produced knowledge is everywhere, doing battle with other kinds of knowledge (produced by personal testimony, opinion, revelation, or rumor) and with other pieces of research-produced knowledge. [18]

This deference to scientific research, profound as it was in North America and Europe, was not universal. Where the state was relatively weak, and where the challenges represented by the global embrace of the market were relatively strong, social science was difficult to organize and sustain. As Miller points out,

> The information society is not being ushered in everywhere. . . . The United States and other industrial countries are information rich and are increasingly able to take advantage of the benefits that new information technologies confer. There are, at the same time, however, many countries that have no access to advanced data and technology resources. This means not only that these countries have fewer informational resources for internal decision-making but also that they may be forced to make international policy and treaty decisions on the basis of inadequate or incomplete information. [19]

What information they did dispose of was often irrelevant to the tasks of public policy.

For many of these countries, capacity-building was a major challenge. With the contraction of the welfare state in the United States and Europe and the collapse of communism in Eastern Europe and Russia, state support of higher education and scientific research was less generous and less secure nearly everywhere. In some parts of the developing world, the assault on the state had started almost before state formation had begun; in those circumstances, social science faced formidable obstacles. In Africa, for example, only two percent of the college age population attended university, and the crisis of the state had produced universities hardly worthy of the name.[20] Few African universities were conducive to social science research, weakened, as the Social Science Research Council reported, by

> dilapidated buildings; an erratic supply of electricity and water; poorly stocked libraries and overcrowded classrooms; shortfall of qualified staff and, because of low salaries, low morale of those who remain; lack of opportunity to do meaningful research; bad management; and a decline in social status and esteem.[21]

In Latin America, the fiscal crisis of the state in the 1980s undermined previously generous state funding for higher education, while in India, the government attempted to compensate for its reduced expenditures on social science research by giving tax breaks for private support of social science research. Elsewhere, public universities were having to reconcile declining budgets with overwhelming demand for higher education from burgeoning populations.

While governments were less eager and less reliable clienteles for university-based social science research, the growing influence of international NGOs and private businesses created new demand for both raw information and refined knowledge about societies, economies, and polities around the world. One measure of this growing demand was the proliferation of private universities, such as the Central European University established in Budapest and Warsaw by the financier George Soros, the Moscow School of Social Sciences, Bilkent and Koc Universities in Turkey, or even the several dozen private universities that had sprung up in Iran in the 1980s and 1990s to accommodate students who did not have access to the more prestigious public universities.[22] In Latin America, private institutions accounted for just over 15 percent of university graduates in 1960; by 1995, the number was 40 percent.[23] In Eastern Europe, Turkey, and much of East Asia, these universities were elite, competitive institutions—English was often the language of instruction—and they were less tradition-bound than their state-supported counterparts, while in Iran and most of Latin America, they served student constituencies—notably women and rural dwellers—who did not have access to public universities. Whether elitist or populist, however, they served to disseminate social science theory and methods to an increasingly wide audience.

Equally significant was the spread not just of social science education but of social science research into institutions well beyond university. For example, Elsbieta Matynia reported that

> there is a fairly vast—and still growing—archipelago of NGO's throughout Central and Eastern Europe that . . . already embraces many new alternative sites for research and training in the social sciences. . . . In this region the NGO is frequently a multipurpose institution, and often operates as a nexus between universities, academics, policy institutes, and publishing houses. [24]

In many parts of the world, for-profit and nonprofit policy-related institutions were multiplying. They employed social scientists to do large volumes of research but, particularly in the absence of robust government-sponsored or university-based social science research establishments, they presented serious challenges to the creation and maintenance of national, or international, social science communities. Nearly everywhere, reliance on private funding was thought to distort research agendas and distract research personnel. Certainly, in both South Asia and Latin America, where the public sector continued to provide institutional support for social science research, even if at a reduced level, the social science communities flourished, not only responding to but also shaping global scholarly agendas, in work on social movements, subaltern studies, and post-coloniality among other arenas. In Eastern Europe, by contrast, it was said that "as domestic funds are currently scarce for any cultural or intellectual work, it is unlikely that much will be produced in social science apart from that which receives foreign sponsorship."[25] In Africa, donor agencies like USAID funded data collection efforts and censuses which usefully employed local social scientists but did not generally reflect local research agendas. Indeed, all African social science was heavily dependent on external funding, especially the Swedish, Canadian, and Dutch development agencies and North American foundations like Ford, Rockefeller, MacArthur, and Carnegie.[26]

The private firms, donors, and development agencies commissioned research and defined the research questions, often producing lucrative but pedestrian findings and draining human and intellectual resources from theoretical or methodological experimentation. Commissioned research was often the property of the funder and if it did not disappear completely, it entered the realm of "grey literature," often circulated but never formally published.

The private market for social research not only set agendas which may not have reflected either the local public interest or a more universal interest in scientific innovation, it also shaped the available labor pool. In Eastern Europe, foreign firms and international financial institutions like the IMF, EBRD, and World Bank recruited social scientists by paying far more than local teaching salaries. In East Asia, many of the best social scientists left the academy for corporate research settings or private-sector positions, in part because the pay scale was higher but also, it was said, because that was "where they feel real-world problems are being addressed."[27]

The retreat of the state and growth of a largely unregulated market for social science research was to mean that in many places there were few institutions charged with supporting and sustaining research communities over time. In Central and Eastern Europe, not only the subjects but even the methods and approaches of the social sciences were shaped by the availability of resources; according to UNESCO, social scientists there were "less likely to employ statistics, modeling and other high powered quantitative methods in large part because of the difficulties in accessing the necessary software programs and computing equipment."[28] In Russia, there was little systematic monitoring or standard-setting. Local and national governments, international NGOs, local and foreign businesses all collected and analyzed data with little or no verification or systematic dissemination of the material they produced. Wide disparities in the quality and credibility of this literature had begun to fuel growing public suspicion of declining standards of research.[29]

Yet, variations in the strength of the state and in its ability to meet or manage the pluralization and internationalization of the sites, sources, and supporters of social science was not the only, nor perhaps even the most important, determinant of the health and vitality of the social scientific research communities. High-quality social science research—and, more important, a continuing commitment to pursuing such research—existed in the face of duress in many countries where the state was weak and society poorly equipped to support it. CODESRIA, the Dakar-based Council for the Development of Social Research in Africa, for example, and the Latin American consortium,

FLACSO, the Facultad Latinoamericana de Ciencas Sociales, represented decades-old regional efforts to provide intellectual and institutional sustenance to social scientists doing high-quality work in sometimes appalling circumstances.[30]

Far more of a challenge was the association of social science with liberalism. As we have seen, American-style social science privileges the individual, relies on freedom of belief and association, and challenges authority. Although these values were upheld as universal, they were not, of course, really so. The cleavage between scientific communities and their societies was apparent even in the United States and it was far deeper in much of the rest of the world. Where literacy was not a foregone conclusion, "numeracy" was often even less common, and in many places, miracles were as likely to define human purpose, identity, and interest as probabilities. There were societies where the market had hardly ever operated and the modern state was virtually unknown. In some of the oil-producing countries of the Arab world, for example, neither the recent past of nomadic pastoralism and regional trade, nor the present of large and somewhat erratic capital windfalls provided much guidance about the workings of a fully developed market, but the oil revenues removed much of the incentive on the part of the government to gather information about the population. Released from the need to tax and able to hire mercenaries, these governments did little to inquire about their subjects. Many people in these countries and in failed states elsewhere, from Afghanistan to Somalia, escaped the reach of the modern bureaucratic administration, with its insatiable desire for information. Even some national governments made policy based not on the research-produced knowledge that presumes social scientific conceptions of human society but on a knowledge that privileges religious revelation, personal intuition, family history, or household networks. Social science had virtually no role in the creation or assessment of public policy in this context, which goes a long way to explain why, for example, in 1998, when asked what the country's inflation rate was, neither the Governor of the Central Bank of Libya nor his director of research knew the answer.[31]

In some places, skepticism about or hostility to scientific methods was less a reflection of what seem to be anachronistic worldviews than of deliberate government policy, as when regimes were reluctant to collect or disseminate information. At the end of the twentieth century, the official population figure for the entire Kingdom of Saudi Arabia was a state secret; half the total volume of economic transactions in Egypt went unrecorded, and there were signs in Iraqi hotels warning citizens not to talk to foreigners. Small wonder that a Gallup poll conducted in nine Muslim countries—itself something of a novelty—and published in February 2002 reported that only 18 percent of respondents said they believed that Arabs had carried out the September 11 attacks.[32]

In these kinds of contexts (and they were prevalent in but by no means limited to the Arab world—after all, it was in Russia that two internationally supported surveys on environmental pollution brought their Russian authors to face charges of treason[33])the work of providing appropriate training, congenial work settings and other institutional support for social science was a profoundly political act. The intimate association of public policy with the liberal assumptions of social science—privileging the individual, relying on free expression and assembly, challenging authority—were more apparent to the world's most autocratic governments than to most of the world's social scientists themselves.[34]

The extent to which this connection between was invisible to American social scientists reflected the extent to which their social science was rooted in the "here and now"—that is, in the United States of the twentieth century. The liberal tradition which shaped social science was not an abstract, transcendent tradition but one that had, as we have seen, a geographical, territorial association. As Kenneth Prewitt has put it,

> The project of American social science has been America. This project, to be sure, has been in some tension with a different project—to build a *science* of politics or economics or psychology. But I believe that a close reading of disciplinary history would demonstrate that the "American project" has time and again taken precedence over the "science project" and that our claims to universal truths are, empirically, very much about the experience of this society in this historical period.[35]

For the social sciences in the United States, approaches to understanding globalization were shaped by the intellectual traditions of international relations and area studies—the contrast between "us" and "everyone else" that was framed at various times by race, by empire, by wars between states (our own and the world's), by the Cold War, by "civilizations"—witness the rhetoric at the end of the twentieth century about "the West and the rest."[36] In this respect, American social scientists required what Americans call "the rest of the world" to provide the definition, by contrast, of their research arena—there is no here and now without there and then. The universalizing ambitions of the social sciences were born in, and reliant on, an imperceptible parochialism.

Thus, both intellectual interests and public policy were to dictate and yet create tensions in systematic inquiry about the far reaches of the globe. In Europe, the imperial mission had provided generous opportunities for social research in the guise of intelligence-gathering about the natives, and many of Europe's most distinguished sociologists and anthropologists—France's Jacques Berque, for example, or Britain's E. E. Evans-Pritchard—made their careers in the service of their nation's empire. Indeed, as John Willensky put it, "the intellectual interests of imperialism could be characterized as reflecting a particular 'will to know.' At its root was a particular desire to take hold of the world, and it was the equal, in its acquisitiveness, to any financial interest in empire."[37] For the United States, imperialism was virtually indistinguishable from state-formation during the nineteenth century, and the "here" simply expanded to obliterate much of the "not-here" as the Western frontier moved across the continent.[38] American social scientists were seduced by the opportunities in empire, however; in 1898, the American Economic Association appointed a committee to develop effective means of administering the U.S. colonies and a number of distinguished economists, including J. W. Jenks and Jacob Hollander, worked on reorganization of the finances of the Philippines and the Puerto Rican treasury and school systems.[39] By the end of World War I, American anthropologists were being recruited into government service on much the same terms as their European counterparts—and creating no small consternation in doing so. In 1919, for example, the noted anthropologist Franz Boas complained in a letter to *The Nation,* that

> By accident, incontrovertible proof has come into my hands that at least four men who carry on anthropological work, while employed as government agents, introduced themselves

to foreign governments as representatives of scientific institutions in the United States, and as sent out for the purpose of carrying on scientific researches. They have not only shaken the belief in the truthfulness of science, but they have also done the greatest possible disservice to scientific inquiry. In consequence of their acts every nation will look with distrust upon the visiting foreign investigator who wants to do honest work, suspecting sinister designs.[40]

By the 1960s, as we have seen, American investigators working abroad encountered precisely the reaction Boaz predicted, although largely as a result of intervening developments.

Indeed, during the interwar period, American social science exhibited relatively little interest in world affairs, save political science's legal and institutional concern with international organization and European government. The American rise to power in World War II revealed the shallowness of American scholarship on the rest of the world, however, and it was to prevent the complacent return to ignorance that had characterized the end of World War I that universities and foundations designed the ambitious postwar architecture for a novel approach to the "not-here" in what became known as "area studies." The building blocks for this project were found partly in the war effort itself, particularly the creation of area experts by the Army and the Navy and the recruitment to the Office of Strategic Services of some of the most prominent university-based social scientists of the day. The Navy located its School of Military Government and Administration, for example—a school designed for the officers who would administer Pacific territories captured from the Japanese—at Columbia University. After the war, the staff of this school, including its director, Schuyler Wallace, would be the nucleus of Columbia's new School of International Affairs. Many university-based social scientists went to Washington; from Columbia alone, the government recruited Ruth Benedict, an anthropologist who prepared her famous book on Japanese culture, *The Chrysanthemum and the Sword*, at the behest of the Office of War Information, Russian historian Geroid Robinson, international relations specialist Grayson Kirk, Russian specialists John Hazard and Philip Mosely, Latin Americanist Bryce Wood, and Middle East expert J. C. Hurewitz, all of whom served in the OSS.[41]

The arguments for the creation of area studies in American universities after the war were several. Not only did the authors of a 1947 Social Science Research Council report suggest that area studies would rectify the overspecialization and parochialism of the social sciences—an almost constant worry in the middle of the twentieth century—they declared that:

> National welfare in the post war period more than ever before requires a citizenry well informed as to other peoples, and the creation of a vast body of knowledge about them. The provincialism of the American public, so often bemoaned, is in no small way, the fault of the American university.[42]

As they had in earlier eras of innovation in the United States, the private foundations played an important role in the initial support of university-based area studies. In 1945, Geroid Robinson, then head of the Eastern European division of OSS, secured a grant of a quarter million dollars from the Rockefeller Foundation for Columbia to establish its Russian Institute. Soon Rockefeller was joined by the Carnegie Corporation and, most importantly, by the Ford Foundation. By the early 1960s, Ford alone had spent more than $100 million in its International Training and Research program to support area studies.[43] In

1959, the Federal government also got into the business of supporting university-based area studies through Title VI of the National Defense Education Act. Much of this was justified by the necessity of confronting communism wherever it might be, a rationale that not only secured resources but also assisted the universities during the onslaught of the McCarthy era.

AREA STUDIES AS AN ALLY OF SOCIAL SCIENCE UNIVERSALISM

The containment of communism also animated one of the most important post-war research agendas in the social sciences: modernization, later known as development, theory. As the subtitle of Walt Rostow's influential *Stages of Economic Growth: A Non-Communist Manifesto* suggested, American social scientists were enlisted in the creation of a theory of social change that would serve the purposes of the multi-pronged battle against communism. The theory that took shape proposed not violent class struggle resulting in proletarian revolution but peaceful, evolutionary reform leading to capitalist prosperity and liberal democracy. Traditional American disdain for history and ignorance of the world were apparent in theoretical formulations that relegated the past to an unchanging and largely invariant "tradition" from which people around the world were presumed to be escaping as quickly as possible in favor of the "modernity" enjoyed by, most notably, the United States itself. The conceptual and empirical problems of this scientific paradigm occupied many of the era's most distinguished minds, as is evident, among other places, in the multivolume project of the Social Science Research Council's Committee on Political Development. It also provided the analytical framework, flawed as it was, that equipped American social scientists to conduct empirical research around the world, and from that research came the armature of the university-based area studies programs. Between the end of the 1940s and the close of the 1980s, thousands of American social scientists spent careers of dual intellectual loyalties, divided between discipline and world region, between the "here" of the social sciences and the "not-here" of area studies.

The political and social upheavals of the 1960s contributed to the collapse of the modernization paradigm. To its credit, however, development theory fell largely under the accumulated weight of empirical knowledge which was a direct result of its own research program, and of the growing connections that American social scientists were forging with social researchers outside the United States. American social science, like so much else in the country, had long been the beneficiary of the brain drain occasioned by strife and poverty elsewhere in the world. [44] The rise of the Nazis in Germany, for example, had produced an infusion of talent most famously into American physics but also into American social science, particularly sociology, and many of the practitioners of area studies had personal associations with the areas they studied: many of the early figures in Middle Eastern studies, for example, were born in the region and educated in Europe before taking up positions in American universities. Starting in the 1970s, however, American social scientists began to collaborate with social researchers who had stayed in, or returned to, their home country after their graduate training. Latin America was the first world region whose social science produced a major contribution to contemporary post–World War II American social science, in the alternative to development approaches to social change known as dependency theory. Dependency theory not only illustrated the existence and sophistication of social theory in Latin America but, in insisting on the importance of history in understanding social phenomena, it also constituted a major challenge to the ahistorical premises of the social science prevalent in the United States. Not least, it had implications for policy, resonating with the post–Vietnam war skepticism about American purposes in the world.

Area studies communities walked a complex and often conflicted line between their purpose as allies of the government in the fight against communism and their growing sympathy with the peoples of the region. The better the area studies scholars knew their regions, the less the imperatives of U.S. foreign policy seemed to capture the aspirations of local populations or the dynamics of regional political and social change. As a result, area studies scholars developed what seemed to be an odd, almost perverse, aversion to working within the prevailing American public policy paradigms. As Robert McCaughey points out, the area studies academics were conspicuous by their absence on both sides of the debates that raged over American foreign policy during the 1960s.[45] Similarly, area studies associations regularly seemed willing to jeopardize the federal funding upon which so many of the university-based area studies research centers relied by contesting the purposes and conditions of government funding. This deliberate distancing from U.S. government policy on the part of American area studies researchers often mystified scholars familiar with other research and policy traditions—particularly those whose governments did not play the global imperial role of the world's superpower.[46] If many area studies social scientists sought to separate themselves from U.S. government policy, unlike their colleagues in the disciplines throughout the 1970 and 1980s, they did not embrace the development of science as an alternative to policy engagement and did little to develop alternative rationales for government and private foundation support of the area studies enterprise. In fact, they were largely unsympathetic to the ambitions of the disciplines to universalist, scientific theory, preoccupied as they were with the particular character of "their" part of the world and aware, if only partly consciously so, of the extent to which American social science was itself an area study. Consider, for example, Prewitt's *American* project.

AREA STUDIES AS IMPEDIMENT TO SOCIAL SCIENCE UNIVERSALISM

When, in the early 1990s, emboldened by the collapse of communism, American social scientists eager to extend the universalizing reach of science expressed impatience with their area studies colleagues, the area studies community, no longer able to take refuge in a national security rationale few of its members had endorsed anyway, was hard put to defend itself. Though numbers rarely tell the whole story, they do reveal something about the vitality of area studies in the United States. For example, in 1990, the major area studies professional associations had 16,000 members—2,000 *fewer* than a decade earlier.[47] The fact that many American policymakers evinced little interest in the rest of the world—recall that one-third of the members of the 1996 U.S. House of Representatives did not even have a passport[48]— also contributed to the sense of loss of purpose experienced by the American area studies community.

Unlike their disciplinary colleagues in the 1960s, who had responded to the disappearance of an easy and comfortable relationship with government policy by turning to an equally reassuring focus on disciplinary progress, many area studies scholars found themselves stymied by the profoundly liberal and often parochial assumptions of their disciplines. American social sciences had from the outset assumed a sort of universal applicability, a benign sense that the "here" which was their concern could expand, like the American frontier, to include anything of interest. Rarely was that assumption tested after the demise of modernization theory, but by the 1990s, a new generation of social scientists felt equipped to try again. The historical association of American social science with liberal public policy, which was all the more powerful for being virtually invisible to its practitioners, was to mean that the American triumphalism that characterized the immediate post–Cold War period would once again be reflected in the universalizing ambitions of American social science.

Despite what should have been one of the principal findings of area studies, the collapse of communism, the end of the Cold War, and the accompanying political and economic transitions from Latin America to Eastern Europe seemed simply to open new opportunities for the social sciences. For social scientists to whom the methods and approaches born in the study of the United States constituted the apex of social scientific achievement, these were fortuitous developments. The institutions of modern political, social, and economic life, for which the instruments of modern political, social, and economic analysis had been devised, were appearing around the world. The fall of communist regimes in eastern Europe and the Soviet Union was seen as creating "virgin territory" for American social scientists interested in market-based economic reform and liberal constitutional design.[49] In economics, for example, neoclassical approaches provided not only a universal analytical lens but also the underpinnings of the global policy prescriptions advocated by the industrialized countries and the international financial institutions—the Washington consensus. In political science, elegant institutional design served not only to affirm the science of formal institutional analysis but also to provide policy recommendations for reform from the Ukraine to Uzbekistan.

Merely a decade later, sobering reminders of the limits of contemporary political and economic science littered the landscape, as the Balkans and Central Asia sank into tyranny and strife while Russia and Southeast Asia faced severe financial crises. As Joseph Stiglitz put it in describing why the IMF had difficulty in constructing effective policy: too much was being made by " a person who stayed in a five star hotel for a few weeks looking at some data." [50] He argued that

> while due obeisance was paid to "political process"—and insights into the political process were often put forward in justification of particular courses for reform—in fact little understanding of these political processes was evidenced. . . . Nor can one separate "principles" from how they are, or are likely to be, implemented. Policy advisors put forth prescriptions in the context of a particular society—a society with a particular history, with a certain level of social capital, with a particular set of political institutions, and with political processes affected by (if not determined by) the existence of particular political forces. Interventions do not occur in a vacuum. [51]

Yet in disciplinary circles, the lessons of failed policy were slow to be drawn and the expanding applicability of apparently universal theoretical approaches seemed virtually a foregone conclusion. In an 1996 issue of the newsletter of the Comparative Politics section of the American Political Science Association, for example, Barry Ames, a noted rational choice theorist, wrote:

> From my perspective as a Latin Americanist, the state of comparative politics looks pretty good. Latin American political

science, at least, is undergoing a renaissance. The return of competitive politics has renewed interest in parties, public opinion, elections, and legislative behavior; the stuff, in other words, of modern political science.[52]

This remarkable equation of the institutions of liberal politics with the research domain of modern political science suggested that authoritarian regimes, kinship networks, kings, cliques, and clients were unfit subjects for systematic political research. American social scientists who worked on regions or countries without established democratic institutions—or, for that matter, fully developed market institutions—found themselves deprived not of only their original policy rationale but even of the promise that they would contribute to scientific advancement.

Nonetheless, American scholars who ventured beyond the transcendent "here" to study politics and economics at the margins of the liberal world had to count themselves fortunate since some of their local counterparts found themselves deprived not only of their scientific authority and policy platform but of their personal freedom as well. In early 2001 Saadeddin Ibrahim, Egypt's most prominent sociologist, and twenty-seven of his colleagues in the Egyptian think tank, the Ibn Khaldun Center for Development Studies, were tried and convicted on charges of having "tarnished" Egypt's image and having received foreign funding—from the European Commission for a documentary film on voter registration—without government authorization. Eighteen moths later, Ibrahim, who was 63 years old and in poor health, was sentenced to seven years at hard labor. This should have served as a warning to all social scientists of the tenuousness of their enterprise. As Mona El-Ghobashy reported,

More than once, the proceedings took on the air of a primer on what research centers do and how they run, reflecting the general lack of awareness and attendant suspicion of these institutions in Egypt. And more than once the defense directed questions to witnesses asking them to clarify the role of a board of directors, the planning of a budget, program evaluation and audit, and the necessity of external funding. Mohammed Al Gohari, former president of Helwan University, explained in his testimony, "If it weren't for foreign funding for scientific and social research in Egypt, we wouldn't have any. Eighty percent of such research is externally bankrolled."[53]

The failure of American social scientists to recognize the different circumstances—intellectual as well as logistical—that their colleagues face around the world not only weakened the quality of international collaboration, but actually impoverished the social science itself.

This ambition to universal social science reflected a haste to generalize against which such collaborations might have been a salutary warning. As Nathan observed,

> the underappreciated danger is that if area studies cease to perform their functions, the disciplines will also cease to perform theirs. Without area studies to take up what is residual to the disciplines, the disciplines will transparently become an area studies of their own, an area studies predominantly of the modern, marketized, democratic West and the times and places where modern and Western values have exerted influence. The disciplines need to get rid not of area studies, but of the idea of situationally uncontaminated or area-neutral data, data from nowhere, just as they have begun to question the idea of the observer from nowhere.[54]

5

Concluding Thoughts
*Social Science, Policymaking, and the Common Good
in the Twenty-first Century*

As we have seen, to some extent the vexed relationship between social science and public policy is congenital, born of the social sciences' parentage in the association of public service and scientific advancement in the United States at the end of the nineteenth century. The oscillation of the American social science community between the orienting axes of public policy and scientific progress for much of the twentieth century reflected both the sustained influence of the Progressivist faith in Woodrow Wilson's apolitical "science of administration" and the anxiety produced by the intrinsic indeterminancy of social science research. Intimately associated with public policy and political power in the early days, social scientists carved out a differentiated professional status in the new research universities at the turn of the twentieth century as scientists distant from the political fray. What was good for science was good for America, and the social sciences were relieved of the obligations of public accountability and political—or moral—responsibility.

Still anxious about their place and power in society, however, social scientists again adopted a public role as the American welfare state and superpower emerged in the emergencies of the Great Depression and World War II. The highwater mark of that state, and of its embrace by social scientists, was in the dual wars of the 1960s, in Vietnam and on Poverty; hurt by the association with these projects, social scientists withdrew once again to their universities, occupying themselves with scientific advancement. A residual aspiration to serve public purposes was apparent only in the reinvention of "the science of administration" in the ostensibly apolitical, technocratic approach to public policy and management that continues to dominate the curriculum of U.S. policy schools.

Yet the withdrawal of the social scientists marked, though it probably did not cause, the beginning of the erosion of the state's monopoly on the definition of the public good, both domestically and internationally. Indeed, today we speak of local and global precisely because the state is no longer alone at the interface between the particular and the universal. The significance of the state in both making public policy and supporting social science—one might even say, in defining the "public" and the "social"—has declined in favor of alternative locations of authority and innovation around the world.

For social scientists, much as they wished to distance themselves from their policy parentage, the fading role of the state was a profound challenge to the enterprise as they had known it, creating multiple sites of public policy and multiple definitions of the public good, and—not incidentally—multiple sources of anxiety about the purposes and power of the social scientist. Their students and their colleagues now worked not only outside the university but beyond government, in myriad think tanks and research departments, consulting firms and business organizations.

Perhaps ironically, public policy issues also provided sites in which interdisciplinary research flourished, albeit in ways that did not always cumulate as either science or policy. Children's health, nuclear nonproliferation, land reform, electoral design, criminal justice, sustainable development, and myriad other policy domains brought together social scientists from a variety of disciplines to work not only with natural scientists and humanists, but also with each other. Sharing a common interest in finding answers to policy questions they considered significant, these social scientists were sometimes impatient with disciplinary self-regard, preferring instead pragmatic and eclectic utilization of a variety of approaches, perspectives, and methods. Disciplinary purists often shuddered at this promiscuity, but it served not only to bring the insights of a variety of disciplines to bear on a pressing social problem, but also to foster mutual understanding, if not appreciation, across the disciplines in the face of the often narrow demands of peer review.

The crowded marketplace of claims, of both audiences and patrons, was further complicated by the fact that it now extended, like markets in so many other things, all over the world. In doing so, it not only increased the variety of ways social science intersected with the public good, but also revealed the parochialism of a science built upon the evidence of one such definition and one such site. Social scientists in much of the rest of the world exhibited little of the anxiety about power and purpose their American colleagues displayed; instead they welcomed opportunities to serve a public purpose. They were not shy about "applied research" or political engagement. In Latin America the 1990s saw what one observer described as "an unprecedented engagement of social scientists with government, with many researchers abandoning academy and research institutions to pursue careers in government and politics." In the

Middle East, the same source observed that "social sciences are linked to public policy debates, which may permit social scientists to be influential as public intellectuals [although] it usually means they are not oriented to the discipline."[1] Arjun Appaduri has asked,

> Is there a principled way to close the gap between many US social scientists, who are suspicious of any form of applied or policy-driven research, and social scientists from many other parts of the world who see themselves as profoundly involved in the social transformations sweeping their own societies?"[2]

Clearly, the historical American relationship between social science and public policy—from the Progressivist enthusiasm for a science of administration to the welfare state's embrace of social engineering—will not govern their relationship in the twenty-first century. The retreat of the state along with the expansion of the arena of policy beyond the public sector and beyond national boundaries have fundamentally reshaped both the supply and the demand for social science. As Craig Calhoun has suggested, we have increasingly come to believe that "a public," including the public for social science, "is not a category of essentially similar people. It is a differentiated body joined, at least in part, by the capacity of its members to sustain a common discourse across their lines of difference."[3] Partly as a result, power is seen to be more widely distributed and more openly contested. Truth is less easily separable—conceptually or politically— from the interests of those who seek and deploy it.

This change in the environment in which public policy is made and implemented poses challenges for social science: no longer do expediency and morality coincide in quite the way they may have a half century ago. The communism of the republic of science, an elitist, often authoritarian conceit among self-regulating "peers," is giving way to arrangements more reminiscent of liberalism's pluralism, to multiple, overlapping communities of researchers. The studied disinterest and skepticism of mid-century science is being superseded by acknowledgment of politics in the often clamorous competition among the private interests of business and the special interests of politics. The aspiration to universalism is now obviously reliant on a once imperceptible parochialism, and with that recognition it has begun to recede in favor of cosmopolitanism, a science that is not merely the projection of the "here" on the "not here" but one that aspires to accommodate the globe's myriad local and national habits and prejudices in commonly acknowledged understanding.

Now that the state does not stand as the sole proxy for power, it is more difficult to argue that truth is separable from power, safe somehow in a protected "apolitical" domain. Just as policy in the twenty-first century depends on the findings of social science, social science itself will increasingly be understood to reflect and rely upon the exigencies of public policy. In fact, there can be no science of society without the organization and the resources of power. The powerful not only select among competing truths, they also shape how we understand what truth itself is. Just as policymakers have come to acknowledge that they understand before they act—that, consciously or not, they have theories and values and analytical assumptions that shape how they proceed— social scientists are acknowledging that they have acted in order to understand. The social sciences' organization of knowledge, choices of problems, selection of analytical tools, definitions of solutions all represent commitments to politically inflected values. For most social scientists, these are the values of American liberalism—both skeptical of and reliant upon the state, embracing the rhetoric of equality and the reality of privilege, confident in the efficacy of human intervention. Whether or not the association of social science with liberalism is to be welcomed, the fact of its existence must be acknowledged before it can be debated, deplored or defended.

We return, however, to the debates that animated our predecessors at the dawn of today's disciplines. For in recognizing the intimate relationship of American liberal values and institutions with the abstract, theoretical, scientific approach to the study of society, we revive the institutionalist perspective with which those predecessors began. Our science itself has been shaped by our values: even as we denied any such influence, our truths have been shaped by how we have understood power. This recognition represents not only a challenge to the social science disciplines as they are presently constituted, but it also returns moral education and public service to center stage—no longer is their link simply a happy byproduct, no longer simply the "coincidence" Robert Merton celebrated.

The changing purposes and parameters of social science and public policy will permit—indeed, require—the reconstitution of their relationship. Universities in the United States and around the world can (indeed will probably be forced to) play a critical role in this reengagement. Even in the face of proliferating sites of research and training, universities remain the principal site for innovation and education in the technical skills of social science research and, more importantly, they are still among the most open and powerful arenas of intellectual contestation, for the elaboration and testing of ideas about the public good. The proliferation of social science in the service of advocacy and the growing presence of think tanks and private research organizations creates special obligations for universities to construct and protect arenas for debate, dissent, and dispute where ideas can be freely tested and refined in the service of wisdom.

Within the university, the policy schools—sites of some of the most important points of connection between the university and its wider world—will have to reflect the changing character of that world. The stylized curriculum of public policy and management of the late twentieth century will have to evolve to transcend the mechanical, scientistic orientation that characterized much instruction and research and the "tools and skill sets" of the policy analyst and manager will have to include recognition of the purposes—the selective purposes born in the perennial struggles over power—to which such skills are put. This requires more than simply reintroducing "political context" courses into the curriculum of the policy schools now content to equip students with ostensibly apolitical analytical tools. As Stiglitz put it, policy "interventions do not occur in a vacuum." Politics is a formative element of policy; indeed it shapes the truths we hold to be self-evident. To understand how this is so, and what other truths may be available to us now, the parochialism of imperial universalism—the projection of the here and now onto other times and places—must be transcended and the domains of knowledge once relegated to anthropology and history reintegrated into public policy research and training. We must recognize that economies—indeed, even the idea of "the economy"—are a reflection of our ideas and institutions as much as they are elements of nature awaiting discovery. Similarly, intimate knowledge of particular localities outside the United States cannot be merely—or even at all—a device to obscure and support the universalist pretensions of American parochialism but must serve to reveal and qualify our ambitions to serve a genuinely common good.

At the beginning of the twenty-first century, in most places around the world, in both their choices of the problems deemed to require a policy response and the solutions they devise to address them, policymakers were typically informed by social science, and through that, by profound, if unwitting, commitment to liberal values. They and their successors would do well to think self-consciously about the links between their tools and techniques and their values and aspirations. This self-consciousness can be fostered in many ways, including exposure to alternatives, in other societies past and present, or perhaps even through familiarity with the peculiar history of social science and public policy itself—a story that should certainly engender appropriate humility.

Research and training in substantive policy arenas—sustainable development; public health and catastrophic emergencies; race, identity and participation; international law and human rights; war, security, and new technologies; urban policy and migration; risk, hazards, and policy planning; institutional design, capacity-building, and democracy—will shape our world, our science, and our policy in the twenty-first century. The social science disciplines will continue to produce methodological innovation but research will also have to reengage policy issues in nondisciplinary or supradisciplinary policy agendas. In doing so, the research and training of public policy makers will not define a universal common good. In transcending specific locales and private interests, however, it will demand and reward commitment to society and public lives in ways at once profoundly different from its nineteenth-century forebears and yet sustained by an explicit confrontation with both truth and power and by a self-conscious commitment to a vision of moral responsibility for the common good. We will once again capture the intimate relationship between the impulses to understand the world and to change it.

Notes

1. INTRODUCTION

1. Richard Stephenson, "Government May Make Private Nearly Half of Its Civilian Jobs," New York Times, November 15, 2002, p. A1.

2. A SCIENCE OF POLITICS

1. Cited in R Gordon Hoxie, *A History of the Faculty of Political Science, Columbia University* (New York; Columbia University Press, 1955), p. 13; also see Julie A. Reuben, *The Making of the Modern University: Intellectual Transformation and the Marginalization of Morality* (Chicago: University of Chicago Press, 1996), p. 160.

2. It went on to say that "The Columbia University Center for the Social Sciences works closely with faculty and students of the MPA program in promoting the use of modern technology and methods for analysis and retrieval of information," emphasizing its connection to Columbia's social science faculty. *Columbia University Bulletin: Graduate Program in Public Affairs and Administration*, 1978–1979, p. 10.

3. Robert K. Merton, "The Role of the Intellectual in Public Bureaucracy," in *Social Theory and Social Structure* Revised edition

(The Free Press of Glencoe, 1957), p. 222. Of course, it was no less an authority than John Maynard Keynes who remarked that "the ideas of economists and political philosophers, both when they are right and when they are wrong, are more powerful than is commonly understood." John Maynard Keynes, *The General Theory of Employment, Interest and Money* (London: MacMillan, 1936), p. 383.

4. Stephen Skrowonek has argued that "professional social science has traditionally played the part of a protagonist in the expansion of American national government." (Stephen Skowronek, *Building a New American State: The Expansion of National Administrative Capabilities, 1877–1920.* (New York: Cambridge University Press, 1982), p. vii. The expansion of the American national government in turn shaped the social sciences themselves.

5. James C. Scott, *Seeing Like a State: How Certain Schemes to Improve to Human Condition have Failed* (New Haven: Yale University Press, 1998), p. 77.

6. Alain Desrosieres, "How to Make Things Which Hold Together: Social Science, Statistics, and the State," in Peter Wagner, Bjorn Wittrock, and Richard Whitley, eds., *Discourses on Society: The Shaping of the Social Sciences* (London: Kluwer Academic Publishers, 1991), p. 91.

7. Scott, *Seeing Like a State*, pp. 91–92.

8. Some years ago, Carl Friedrich gave us an interpretation, typical in its convoluted carefulness, of what the word "policy" has meant to most students of the subject. Policy is " . . . a proposed course of action of a person, group or government within a given environment providing obstacles and opportunities which the policy was proposed to utilize and overcome in an effort to reach a goal or realize an objective or a purpose." Carl J. Friedrich, *Man and His Government* (New York: McGraw-Hill, 1963), p. 79.

9. Walter W. Powell, and Elisabeth S. Clemens, *Private Action and the Public Good* (New Haven: Yale University Press, 1998), pp. xiii–xiv.

10. Anthony Cordesman, "Transitions in the Middle East," an address to the 8th US Mideast Policymakers Conference, September 9, 1999. Http://www.csis.org/mideast/reports/ transitions.html.

11. Webster's Unabridged tells us that "science" is "systemized knowledge derived from observation, study and experimentation carried on in order to determine the nature or principles of what is being studied." No doubt it is, although book reviewer Richard Eder's recent description of science's "churning hunger to see beyond what can be seen" evokes the temper of the scientific enterprise somewhat more elegantly. "Up the Garden Path," *The New York Times Book Review*, August 13, 2000.

12. John Stuart Mill, *Some Unsettled Questions of Political Economy,*" 1844, p. 180.

13. Peter Hall, "Policy Paradigms, Experts, and the State: The Case of Macroeconomic Policy-Making in Britain" in Stephen Brooks and Alain-G. Gagnon, eds., *Social Scientists, Policy, and the State* (New York: Praeger, 1990), p. 62.

14. Richard Whitley, *The Intellectual and Social Organization of the Sciences* 2nd edition (Oxford: Oxford University Press, 2000), p. 6.

15. National Science Foundation documents cited in R. C. Lewontin, "The Cold War and the Transformation of the Academy," in Noam Chomsky, et al., *The Cold War and the University: Toward an Intellectual History of the Postwar Years* (New York: The New Press, 1997), p. 34.

16. Johan Heilbron, "The Tripartite Division of French Social Science: A Long-Term Perspective," in Wagner, et al., eds., *Discourses on Society*, p. 78.

17. Cited in Dorothy Ross, *The Origins of American Social Science,* (Cambridge: Cambridge University Press, 1991), p. 59.

18. Ross, *The Origins of American Social Science*, p. 161.

19. Lawrence R. Veysey, *The Emergence of the American University* (Chicago: University of Chicago Press, 1965), p. 12.

20. Julie A. Reuben, *The Making of the Modern University,* p. 157.

21. Jean Bethke Elshtain, "Why Public Intellectuals?" *The Wilson Quarterly,* 25: 4 (Autumn 2001): 44.

22. In Europe, reformers were less attached to universities, although one of the best-known reform movements in Victorian England was the Fabian Society, which was instrumental in the establishment of the London School of Economics. Bjorn Wittrock and Peter Wagner, "Social Science Developments: The Structuration of Discourse in the Social Sciences," in Stephen Brooks and Alain-G. Gagnon, eds., *Social Scientists, Policy, and the State* (New York: Praeger, 1990), p. 119.

23. Ross, *The Origins of American Social Science,* p. 70.

24. Gulbenkian Commission, *Open the Social Sciences; Report of the Gulbenkian Commission on Restructuring the Social Sciences* (Stanford: Stanford University Press, 1996), p. 17. Economist Robert Solow observes about this vision: "'To the extent that economists have the ambition to behave like physicists, they face two dangerous pitfalls. The first is the temptation to believe that the laws of economics are like the laws of physics: exactly the same everywhere on earth and at every moment since Hector was a pup. That is certainly true about the behavior of heat and light. But the part of economics that is independent of history and social context is not only small but dull." Robert M. Solow, "How Did Economics Get That Way and What Way Did It Get?" in Thomas Bender and Carl E. Schorske, eds., *American Academic Culture in Transformation: Fifty Years, Four Disciplines* (Princeton: Princeton University Press, 1997), p. 74. See also, Timothy Mitchell, "Fixing the Economy," *Cultural Studies* 12:1, 1998.

25. Cited in Said Amir Arjomand, "International Sociology into the New Millennium," *International Sociology,* 15:1 (March 2000): 5.

26. Gulbenkian Commission, p. 20.

27. As Cohn put it, "in a very real way, the subject matter of anthropology has been the study of the colonized.' (Bernard Cohn,

"The Census, Social Structure, and Objectification in South Asia," in *An Anthropologist Among the Historians and other Essays* (Oxford: Oxford University Press, 1987), p. 224.

28. John G. Gunnell, "In Search of the State: Political Science as an Emerging Discipline in the U.S." in Wagner, et al, eds., *Discourses on Society*, p. 152, citing Frank Goodnow and Henry Jones Ford in the *Proceedings of the American Political Science Association*, 1905, 1906.

29. Ross, *The Origins of American Social Science*, p. 63.

30. Woodrow Wilson, "The Study of Administration," *Political Science Quarterly* 2:2 (June 1887): 201; Ross, *The Origins of American Social Science*, p. 158.

31. Peter Manicas, "The Social Science Disciplines: The American Model," in Wagner, et all, eds., *Discourses on Society*, p. 58; Rebecca S. Lowen, *Creating the Cold War University: The Transformation of Stanford* (Berkeley: University of California Press, 1997), p. 22.

32. Wittrock and Wagner, "Social Science Developments," p.121.

33. Robert Vitalis, "International Studies in America," unpublished paper, 2002, p. 23.See also his "The Graceful and Generous Liberal Gesture: Making Racism Invisible in American International Relations," *Millenium: Journal of International Studies*, 29:2, 2000 .

34. Heilbron, "Tripartite Division of French Social Science,", p. 78.

35. Gunnell, "In Search of the State," p.145.

36. Wilson, "The Study of Administration," p. 202.

37. Ross , *The Origins of American Social Science,* p. 255.

38. Cited in Ibid., p. 403.

39. Whitley, *The Intellectual and Social Organization of the Sciences,* p. 11.

40. Carl E. Schorske, "The New Rigorism in the Human Sciences, 1940–1960," in Thomas Bender and Carl E. Schorske, eds., *American Academic Culture in Transformation,* p. 317; Anthony Giddens, *The Nation-State and Violence* (Cambridge: Polity Press, 1985), p. 181. See also the introduction of David H. Guston, *Between Science*

and Politics: Assuring Integrity and Productivity of Research (Cambridge: Cambridge University Press, 1999), for a nuanced discussion of the character of the natural sciences.

41. Merton, "The Role of the Intellectual in Public Bureaucracy," p. 211 As Peter Hall puts it, "social science will rarely be able to validate a new set of ideas on scientific grounds alone; and policy makers are unlikely to adopt a new set of ideas simply because they reflect the most recent findings of social science." Hall, "Policy Paradigms, Experts, and the State," p. 61.

42. Robert Dahl, for example, echoes this concern, "No intellectually defensible claim can be made that public policy elites (actual or putative) possess superior moral knowledge or more specifically superior knowledge of what constitutes the public good. Indeed, we may have some reason for thinking that specialization itself may impair their capacity for moral judgement. Likewise, precisely because the knowledge of policy elites is specialized, their expert knowledge ordinarily provides too narrow a base for the instrumental judgements that an intelligent policy would require." (Robert Dahl, *Democracy and its Critics* (New Haven: Yale University Press, 1989), p. 337).

43. Ross, *The Origins of American Social Science*, p. 161.

44. The ties between liberal (as opposed to progressive) political agendas, private foundations, and experiments in the institutionalization of social science are evident in the early history of the New School for Social Research, founded in 1918 by left-wing Progressive social scientists, including Charles Beard, who had just been dismissed from Columbia, and his colleagues John Dewey, and Thorstein Veblen. They too wanted to promote scientific social research but because of their social democratic leanings, they did not receive significant support from the private foundations. As a result, the faculty dispersed and the New School turned to adult education and to culture rather than social science. (see Ross, *The Origins of American Social Science*, p. 404).

45. Beardsley Ruml, cited in Kenton W. Worcester, "The Social Science Research Council, 1923–1998," unpublished manuscript, p. 10.

46. Ibid., p. 17.

47. In the 1934–35 academic year, $11.5 million was dispersed by the Federal Relief Administration to support 100,000 students at 1,450 colleges and universities. See Lowen, *Cold War University*, p. 31; Robert A. Heineman, et al., *The World of the Policy Analyst: Rationality, Values and Politics* (Chatham, NJ: Chatham House Publishers, 1997), p. 15.

48. Desrosieres, "How to Make Things," p. 209.

49. Mitchell, forthcoming, p. 13.

50. Lowen, *Cold War University*, p. 76.

51. Schorske, "The New Rigorism in the Human Sciences," p, 316. That there was some dispute about the character of the research produced is suggested in the story Alexander George tells of Dean Acheson's reaction to a scholarly study of his role in early U.S. involvement in the Korean war. Acheson objected to being treated as a dependent variable, says George, for he considered himself to have been an independent variable in that crisis. (George, *Bridging the Gap: Theory and Practice in Foreign Policy* (Washington: United States Institute of Peace Press, 1993), p. 7.

52. Thomas Bender, "Politics, Intellect, and the American University, 1945–1995," in Bender and Schorske, eds., *American Academic Culture in Transformation*, p. 23.

53. Ira Katznelson, "The Subtle Politics of Developing Emergency: Political Science as Liberal Guardianship," in Noam Chomsky, et al., *The Cold War and the University: Toward an Intellectual History of the Postwar Years* (New York: The New Press, 1997), p. 238.

54. Bender, "Politics, Intellect," p. 21.

55. Louis Menand, "Undisciplined," *The Wilson Quarterly*, 25: 4(Autumn 2001): 55.

56. Gary Sick observes that "the MacNamara revolution at the Pentagon in the 1960s, when he brought the Whiz Kids in and challenged the existing bureaucracy with modern management and operations research techniques, was a part of this marriage of social science and public policy. At first, the generals and admirals simply

resisted, but they quickly realized they were going to lose the battle, so they began training their own cadre of PhDs to be able to compete on his terms. They were less interested in what their people studied than they were in having people around who could use the jargon and the techniques of modern social science. Among other things, they sponsored academic programs for younger officers to get PhDs, with only minimal concern about the actual subject matter—within reason. . . . In the process, it did change the way the armed services talked and even, eventually, the way they organized themselves and fought wars." (Personal communication, October 2000).

57. Cited in Lowen, *Cold War University*, p, 147.

58. Leslie Pal, "Knowledge, Power and Policy: Reflections on Foucault" in Brooks and Gagnon, eds., *Social Scientists, Policy, and the State*, p. 141.

59. As Robert McCaughey has pointed out, during 60s and 70s, "international studies academics, particularly on campuses most heavily involved with the petition campaigns and teach-ins, were conspicuous by their avoidance of both. . . . the decision to sign or not to sign a public statement on the war involved more than a personal judgement on the war. It also involved the professional implications of engaging on either side of a public debate on issues about which [the academic] lay claim to expertise. (Robert A. McCaughey, *International Studies and Academic Enterprise: A Chapter in the Enclosure of American Learning* (New York: Columbia University Press 1984), p. 233.

60. See Immanuel Wallerstein, "The Unintended Consequences of Cold War Area Studies," in Chomsky et al., *The Cold War and the University*; Irving Louis Horowitz, ed., *The Rise and Fall of Project Camelot* (Cambridge: MIT Press, 1967) .

61. Paul F. Lazarsfeld, "The Policy Sciences Movement (An Outsider's View)," *Policy Sciences* 6, 1975.

62. Bender, "Politics, Intellect," p. 29.

63. E. Roy Weintraub, *How Economics Became a Mathematical Science*, Durham: Duke University Press, 2002, pp. 24–7, 255.

64. As Whitley points out, in the 1950s, half of all American PhDs in economics were produced by Berkeley, Chicago, Columbia, Harvard, MIT and Wisconsin. The job market for these PhDs reflected the enormous increase in higher education; two-thirds of them landed academic jobs. (Whitley, *The Intellectual and Social Organization of the Sciences*, p. 248) .

65. Alain-G. Gagnon, "The Influence of Social Scientists on Public Policy," in Brooks, Stephen and Gagnon, eds., *Social Scientists, Policy, and the State* , p. 2; Schorske, "The New Rigorism in the Human Sciences" p. 326.

66. Edward Said, *Beyond the Academy: A Scholar's Obligations* American Council of Learned Societies Occasional Paper, # 31, 1995, p. 31.

67. Werner Jann, "From Policy Analysis to Political Management: An Outside Look at Public-Policy Training in the United States," in Peter Wagner, et al., eds., *Social Sciences and Modern States: National Experiences and Theoretical Crossroads* (Cambridge: Cambridge University, Press 1991), quoting Herbert Simon on business schools, p. 120.

68. Jann, "Policy Analysis to Pollitical Management," p. 111.

69. As Charles Lindblom pointed out, "staff members . . . need to be educated or trained better to understand just what character of problem it is that their politician-employers face." (Charles E. Lindblom, "Political Science in the 1940s and 1950s" in Bender, Thomas and Carl E. Schorske, eds., *American Academic Culture in Transformation: Fifty Years, Four Disciplines* (Princeton: Princeton University Press, 1997), p. 249–250). See also James S. Coleman, *Policy Research in the Social Sciences* (Morristown, NJ: General Learning Press, 1972), on the differences between what he calls "discipline research" and "policy research" in the social sciences.

70. Jann, "Policy Analysis to Pollitical Management," p. 118.

71. I am grateful to Steve Solnick for this insight.

72. Cited in Paul Primack, "Private Gain, Public Loss: Why Policy Students Opt Out of Government Service," Working Paper 2,

Rappaport Insitute for Greater Boston, John F. Kennedy School of Government, Harvard University, 2000, p. 15.

73. Scott, *Seeing Like a State*, p. 4.

74. As Pierre Bourdieu suggests, "formalisms of all stripe are often the gilded cage in which those who are free to say anything at all imprison themselves, provided that they say nothing about anything essential or that they say it in such a form that nothing will escape the closed circle of the initiated. (Pierre Bourdieu, "The Peculiar History of Scientific Reason," *Sociological Forum* 6:1 (1991): 20).

75. Craig Calhoun, "The Public Good as a Social and Cultural Project," in Powell and Clemens, *Private Action and the Public Good*, p. 32.

76. Whitley, *The Intellectual and Social Organization of the Sciences* p. 232.

3. A MARKETPLACE OF IDEAS

1. World Bank, *Claiming the Future: Choosing Prosperity in the Middle East and North Africa* (Washington, DC, 1995), p. 14.

2. Gretchen Morgenson, "A Company Worth More than Spain?" The *New York Times,* December 26, 1999.

3. Claudia H. Deutsch, "Unlikely Allies With the United Nations," *The New York Times*, December 10, 1999.

4. Sandrine Tesner, with the collaboration of George Kell, *The United Nations and Business: A Partnership Recovered* (New York: St. Martin's Press, 2000), p. 26; see also United Nations, *The Global Compact*, nd; www.un.org/partners/business.

5. P. W. Singer, "Corporate Warriors: The Rise of the Privatized Military Industry and Its Ramifications for International Security," *International Security* Winter 2001–01.

6. Powell and Clemens, *Private Action and the Public Good,* p. xv; Lester M. Salamon et al, *Global Civil Society: Dimensions of the Nonprofit Sector* (Baltimore: The Johns Hopkins Center for Civil Society Studies, 1999), p. 13.

7. Diane Stone, *Capturing the Political Imagination: Think Tanks and Policy Processes* (London: Frank Cass, 1996), p. 18.

8. Brian Whitaker, "US Thinktanks Give Lessons in Foreign Policy," *The Guardian*, August 19, 2002.

9. David L. Featherman and Maris A. Vinovskis, eds., *Social Science and Policy-Making: A Search for Relevance in the Twentieth Century* (Ann Arbor: University of Michigan, 2001), p. 2. See also pp. 65–67.

10. James G. McGann and R. Kent Weaver, eds., *Think Tanks and Civil Societies: Catalysts for Ideas and Action* (New Brunswick: Transaction Publishers, 2000), p, 3.

11. Powell and Clemens, *Private Action and the Public Good*, p. xv.

12. Primack, "Private Gain, Public Loss," p.1.

13. Philip G. Attach, "Private-Sector Shift In Education Serves More Students but Alters Cost and Quality," *The World Paper*, January/February 2000, p. 7.

14. Bernd Waechter, "European Universities Must Adapt in an Era of Global Competition," *The Chronicle of Higher Education*, December 7, 2001, p. B24.

15. UNESCO, *World Social Science Report 1999* (Paris: UNESCO/Elsevier, 1999), p. 158.

16. See Robert Merton's astute and very funny musings on the fate of one of his coinages—"the self-fulfilling prophecy." in "Our Sociological Vernacular," *Columbia: the Magazine of Columbia University*, November 1981.

17. Joseph Duffey, "Mortarboard Multinationals," *The World Paper* January/February 2000, p. 7. Of the twenty-four year olds in the mid-1980s, 24% of Americans had a college degree, as did 22% of the Japanese, 15% of the French, 14% of the British, and 12% of the Germans. See Roger M. Noll, ed., *Challenges to Research Universities* (Washington: Brookings Institution Press, 1998), p. 13.

18. Pal, "Knowledge, Power and Policy: Reflections on Foucault," p. 143.

19. For a historical treatment of this question, see Alfred W. Crosby, *The Measure of Reality: Quantification and Western Society, 1250–1600,* (Cambridge: Cambridge University Press, 1997).

20. *The New York Times Magazine,* July 23, 2000.

21. See David Leonhardt, "In Football 6+2 Often Equals 6," *The New York Times* January 16, 2000, section 4, p. 2.

22. Indeed, even my then ten-year son speculated about what "his generation" would be called; this is Anthony Gidden's "reflexive monitoring of action," which he argues is an inherent part of contemporary society. See UNESCO, *World Social Science Report 1999,* p. 85.

23. Whitley, *The Intellectual and Social Organization of the Sciences,* p. 238.

24. Gagnon, "The Influence of Social Scientists on Public Policy,", p. 7.

25. Henry Etzkowitz, et al., "Academia, Interrupted: Normative Change in Science" unpublished paper, p. 8, see also Noll, *Challenges to Research Universities..*

26. David Hart, "The Changing Governance of Technological Innovation: Internationalization, Privatization, Federalization," unpublished paper, July 9, 1997; Whitley, *The Intellectual and Social Organization of the Sciences,* p.xx..

27. Quoted in Jonathan Karp, "Change of course: India's Ivory Towers Try to Get Practical," *Far Eastern Economic Review,* November 14, 1996.

28. Arthur Lupia, "Evaluating Political Science Research: Information for Buyers and Sellers," *PS,* March 2000, p. 7.

29. See for example, the debates that raged in the area studies associations about the propriety of accepting funding from the National Security Education Program, a fellowship program created in 1991 to "increase the ability of Americans to communicate and compete globally by knowing the languages and cultures of other countries." Because it was funded through a Congressional appropriation from the defense and intelligence budgets, and was administered by the Department of Defense, rather than the Department of Education,

which was the historical administrative home of federal programs to support area studies, many area studies and other scholarly associations objected, citing the possibility that the program would jeopardize American scholars conducting research abroad. See Stanley J. Heginbotham, "The National Security Education Program," *Items,* Social Science Research Council, 46:2–3 (June-September 1992); and the websites of the principal area studies associations, such as www.mesa.arizona.edu.

30. William J. Barber, "Reconfigurations in American Academic Economics: A General Practitioner's Perspective," in Bender and Schorske, eds., *American Academic Culture in Transformation*, p. 116.

31. Andrew Webster and Henry Etzkowitz, "Toward a Theoretical Analysis of Academic-Industry Collaboration," in Henry Etzkowitz, Andrew Webster, and Peter Healey, eds. *Capitalizing Knowledge: New Intersections of Industry and Academia* (Albany: State University of New York Press, 1998), p. 60.

32. Paul A. Beck, et al., "Planning Our Future: The Report of the American Political Science Association's Strategic Planning Committee," *PS: Political Science and Politics* 33:4 (December 2000): 881.

33. A sampling of the sentiment is printed in Ibid.

34. Valerie Martinez-Ebers et al, in Ibid., p. 895.

35. Frank Sorauf, et al., "Political Science at the NSF: The Report of a Committee of the American Political Science Association," Ibid., p. 896–897.

36. Cited in "Marburger Declares Importance of Social Sciences," *COSSA Washington Update* Consortium of Social Science Associations, 21:7, April 15, 2002.

37. The APSA is, as the legal jargon has it, a 501(c)3 charity. See Paul Beck et al., "Planning Our Future," p. 880.

38. Whitley, *The Intellectual and Social Organization of the Sciences*, p. xviii.

39. Merton, "The Role of the Intellectual in Public Bureaucracy," In *Social Theory and Social Structure*, revised edition (Glencoe: The Free Press, 1957 [1945]), p. 553.

40. Ibid, p 557.

41. Scott, *Seeing Like a State,* p. 335 Perhaps better, it is inalienable—that is, it cannot be reassigned from its source. Thanks to Jon Anderson for pointing out this ambiguity.

42. Michael Aaron Dennis, "Secrecy and Science Revisited: From Politics to Historical Practice and Back," in Judith Reppy, ed., *Secrecy and Knowledge Production* Cornell Peace Studies Program, Occasional Paper #23, October 1999, p.4.

43. Robert K. Merton, "The Matthew Effect in Science, II: Cumulative Advantage and the Symbolism of Intellectual Property," *ISIS*, 1988, p. 620.

44. Dennis, "Secrecy and Science Revisited," p. 11.

45. Paul Evans, personal communication 1999.

46. Whitley, *The Intellectual and Social Organization of the Sciences, op, cit.,* p.51; see also John Ziman, *Real Science: What It Is, and What It Means* (Cambridge: Cambridge University Press, 2000), p. 116.

47. Etzkowitz, "Academia Interrupted," p. 2.

48. See John Palattella, "May the Course Be With You: Universities Claim the Right to Sell Classes on the Internet. The Faculty Strikes Back." *Lingua Franca* March 2001.

49. Peter Evans, "The Eclipse of the State? Reflections on Stateness in an Era of Globalization," *World Politics* 50, October 1997, p. 78.

50. Evert A. Lindquist, "The Third Community, Policy Inquiry, and Social Scientists," in Brooks and Gagnon, eds., *Social Scientists, Policy, and the State* , p. 30.

51. Ibid., p. 79; George, *Bridging the Gap,* p. 10.

52. Richard A. Caldwell, ed. *Public Policy Resource Guide* (Denver: University of Denver Institute for Public Policy Studies, 2002), p. 1.

53. Edward Muir, "They Blinded Me with Political Science: On the Use of Non Peer-Reviewed Research on Education Policy," *PS: Political Science and Politics* 32:4 (December 1999).

54. Mitchell, forthcoming, p. 27.

55. Patricia Cohen, "Oops, Sorry: My Pie Chart Seems to be Half-Baked," *The New York Times*, April 8, 2000, p. B7.

56. Etzkowitz, "Academia Interrupted," p. 3.

57. Charles R. Hale, "What is Activist Research?" *Items and Issues*, Social Science Research Council 2:1–2 (Summer 2001): 13.

58. Robert K. Merton, "A Note on Science and Democracy," *Journal of Legal and Political Sociology* 1 (1942): 556.

59. Scott, *Seeing Like a State*, p. 94.

60. Cited by Dennis, "Secrecy and Science Revisited," p. 13.

61. Nell Irwin Painter, "Black Studies, Black Professors, and the Struggles of Perception," *The Chronicle of Higher Education* December 15, 2000, p. B7.

62. David Block, *Assessing Scholarly Communication in the Developing World: It takes More Than Bytes*, SSRC Working Paper Series on Building Intellectual Capicity for the 21st Century, New York: SSRC, 2001, p. 4.

63. Bender, "Politics, Intellect," p. 46.

64. "The character of the schools seems to depend strongly on . . . characteristics of the American polity and culture. The polity places importance on professional training, on economic reasoning, and quantitative data. Very roughly, the 'administrative culture' or 'policy-making style' in the United States can be characterized as more fragmented and short-term oriented than, say, in Germany, where legal correctness, procedure, and the right to act are at least as important as effectiveness and efficiency and where institutions are more important than persons. . . . Public policy schools are closely connected to the values inherent in pluralism, incrementalism, and the 'free market system.'"(Jann, "Policy Analysis to Political Management," pp. 123–25).

65. See, for example, Chris Hedges, "New Activists are Nurtured by Politicized Curriculums," *The New York Times* May 27, 2000.

66. Lindblom, "Political Science in the 1940s and 1950s," p. 265.

67. Cited in Bender, "Politics, Intellect," p. 47.

68. Calhoun, "The Public Good as a Social and Cultural Project," p. 33.

4. WARS AND WEBS

1. David Held, et al *Global Transformations: Politics, Economics, and Culture* (Stanford: Stanford University Press, 1999), p. 1

2. Malcolm Vout, "Oxford and the Emergence of Political Science in England, 1945–1960," in Wagner, et al., eds., *Discourses on Society*, p. 166.

3. Wallerstein, "Unintended Consequences," p. 224.

4. Peter Wagner and Bjorn Wittrock, "States, Institutions, and Discourses: A Comparative Perspective on the Structuration of the Social Sciences," in Wagner, et al., eds., *Discourses on Society*, p. 333.

5. Mamdani, Mahmood, "Africa and African Studies," unpublished manuscript, 2001.

6. Arjomand, "International Sociology," p. 6.

7. Fred Halliday, "The Chimera of the 'International University,'" *International Affairs,* 75:1 (1999): 102; UNESCO, *World Social Science Report 1999*, p. 61.

8. See at http://education.guardian.co.uk.

9. Roberta Balstead Miller, "The Information Society: O Brave New World," *Social Science Computer Review* 13:2 (Summer 1995): 165.

10. Barber, "Reconfigurations in American Academic Economics, p. 116; http://www.pub.whitehouse.gov/uri-r . . . //oma.eop.gov.us/2000/4/20/3.text.

11. Whitley, *The Intellectual and Social Organization of the Sciences,* p. 132.

12. Arjomand, "International Sociology," pp. 8–9.

13. Halliday, "The Chimera of the 'International University,'" p.100.

14. Wittrock and Wagner, "Social Science Developments," pp. 124, 132.

15. Ibid. p. 133.

16. UNESCO, *World Social Science Report 1999t*, p. 89.

17. Jann, "Policy Analysis to Pollitical Management," p.111.

18. Arjun Appadurai, "The Research Ethic and the Spirit of Internationalism," *Items* (Social Science Research Council) 51:4, Part I (December 1997): 58; Carol Weiss agrees: "Policymakers who consciously pay attention to social science view themselves, and are often viewed by others, as behaving rationally. It is often in their interest to commission studies, call in experts, and cite social science evidence. This shows their colleagues and the public that they are good decisionmakers because they are abiding by the convention to study the facts." Carol H. Weiss, "The Uneasy Partnership Endures: Social Science and Government," in Steven Brooks and Alain-G. Gagnon, *Social Scientists, Policy and the State* (New York: Praeger, 1990), p. 101.

19. R. B. "The Information Society," p. 167.

20. Dan Carnevale, "World Bank Becomes a Player in Distance Education," *The Chronicle of Higher Education,* December 8, 2000, p. A36.

21. Kenneth Prewitt, *Networks in International Capacity Building: Cases from Sub-Saharan Africa,* (New York: SSRC, 1998), p. 19; see also Burton Bollag, "Chaos on African Campuses," *The Chronicle of Higher Education,* July 12, 2002.

22. David Cohen, "The Worldwide Rise of Private Colleges," *The Chronicle of Higher Education*, March 9, 2001, p. A47.

23. Monique Segarra, personal communication.

24. Elzbieta Matynia, personal communication.

25. Joan Roelofs and Erkki Berndtson, "Foundations, Social Scientists and Eastern Europe," in Brooks and Gagnon, eds., *The Political Influence of Idea*, p. 182.

26. UNESCO, *World Social Science Report 1999*, p.127; see also Burton Bollag, "An African Success Story at the U. of Dar es Salaam," *The Chronicle of Higher Education,* April 6, 2001, p. A53.

27. UNESCO, *World Social Science Report 1999*, pp. 95, 142.

28. Ibid, p.100.

29. Ibid, p.101.

30. On FLACSO, established in 1957, see http://www.flacso.org; on CODESRIA, founded in 1973, see http://www.sas.upenn.edu/ African_Studies/codesria/codes_Menu.html. On the challenges of scholarly research in war zones, see Michael Easterbrook, "Murders and Threats Plague Colombia's Universities," *The Chronicle of Higher Education*, November 2, 2001; Lisa Anderson, "Social Science Under Duress," published as "Las ciencias socials bajo presión," *Revista de Economía Institucional* #2, primer semestre 2000, pp. 197–206.

31. "Libya: Mystery of the Vanishing Money" *The Economist*, February 7, 1998.

32. Http://www.usatoday.com/news/attack/2002/02/27/usat-poll.htm.

33. UNESCO, *World Social Science Report 1999*, p. 100.

34. "To be a social scientist in the Middle East is, in some contexts, equivalent to associating oneself with an entire set of highly politicized positions. These concern public policy debates on issues such as gender relations, family planning, health and welfare policies, as well as concerns relating to the relationship between the Muslim world and the West; how to explain social change; and whether agency is situated within individuals or in the demands of the Islamic faith. To be social scientist is often perceived as a commitment to modernisms of varying forms, and is often counterposed to 'being Muslim' . . . " Ibid, p. 104.

35. Kenneth Prewitt, "The Social Science Project: Then, Now and Next," *Items and Issues*, Social Science Research Council, 3:1–2 (Spring 2002): 6.

36. See Samuel P. Huntington, *The Clash of Civilizations and the Remaking of the World Order* (New York: Simon & Schuster, 1996) .

37. John Willinsky, *Learning to Divide the World: Education at Empire's End*, (Minneapolis: University of Minnesota Press, 1998), p. 26.

38. An observation I owe to Robert Vitalis.

39. Manicas, "The Social Science Disciplines," pp .57–58.

40. Boas, "Scientists as Spies," in Christopher Simpson, ed., *Universities and Empire: Money and Politics in the Social Sciences during the Cold War* (New York: The New Press, 1998), p. 2.

41. McCaughey, *International Studies and Academic Enterprise*," pp. 116–120.

42. Robert B. Hall, *Area Studies, with Special Reference to Their Implications for Research in the Social Sciences* (New York, Social Science Research Council, 1947), cited in Wallerstein,"Unintended Consequences," p..202.

43. McCaughey, *International Studies and Academic Enterprise*, p.192.

44. See Kim McDonald, "U.S. Dominates Nobel Prizes in Science, but All Its Winners Are Foreign Born," *The Chronicle of Higher Education,* October 22, 1999, p. A23.

45. McCaughey, *International Studies and Academic Enterprise,* p. 232.

46. Most recently, Martin Kramer, in *Ivory Towers on Sand: The Failure of Middle Eastern Studies in America* (Washington, DC: The Washington Institute for Near East Policy, 2001).

47. Gilbert W. Merkx, "Area and International Studies and Its Stakeholders," in Neil J. Smelser and Paul J. Baltes, *International Encyclopedia of the Social and Behavioral Sciences* (Oxford: Elsevier Science Limited, 2001), p. 2.

48. *International Herald Tribune*, May 6, 1998.

49. This term was used without irony by a prominent American social scientist whom I will not embarrass by identifying.

50. Quoted in Moberg, David, "Silencing Joseph Stiglitz," *Salon.com,* May 2, 2000, http://www.salon.com/news/feature/2000/05/02/stiglitz, p. 2.

51. Joseph E. Stiglitz, "Whither Reform? Ten Years of Transition," Keynote address for the World Bank Annual Conference on Development Economics, Washington DC, April 28–30, 1999, p. 4; see also Joseph E. Stiglitz *Globalization and Its Discontents* 2002.

52. Barry Ames, "Comparative Politics and the Replication Controversy," *APSA-CP: Newsletter of the APSA Organized Section on Comparative Politics* 17:1 (Winter 1997): 12.

53. Mona El-Ghobashy, "The case against Saad Eddin Ibrahim reveals deep-seated suspicions about the nature of social research," *Cairo Times* January 24, 2001: see also Mary Anne Weaver, "Egypt on Trial" *The New York Times Magazine*, June 17, 2001.

54. Andrew J. Nathan, "Universalism: A Particularistic Account," in Lynda S. Bell, Andrew J. Nathan, and Ilan Peleg, eds., *Negotiating Culture and Human Rights* (New York: Columbia University Press, 2001), p. 364.

5. CONCLUDING THOUGHTS

1. UNESCO, *World Social Science Report 1999*, pp. 199, 108, 138

2. Appaduri, "The Research Ethic," p. 59

3. Calhoun, "The Public Good as a Social and Cultural Project," p. 30

References

Ames, Barry. "Comparative Politics and the Replication Controversy." *APSA-CP: Newsletter of the APSA Organized Section on Comparative Politics* 17:1 (Winter 1997).

Anderson, Lisa. "Politics in the Middle East: Opportunities and Limits in the Quest for Theory." In Mark Tessler, ed. *Area Studies and Social Science: Strategies for Understanding Middle East Politics*. Bloomington: Indiana University Press, 1999.

————. "Social Science Under Duress." Published as "Las ciencias socials bajo presión," *Revista de Economía Institucional* #2, primer semestre 2000.

Appadurai, Arjun. "The Research Ethic and the Spirit of Internationalism." *Items*. (Social Science Research Council) 51:4, Part I, December 1997.

"APSA Celebrates its Centennial." *PS: Political Science & Politics* 31:2, June 1998.

Arjomand, Said Amir. "*International Sociology* into the New Millennium." *International Sociology* 15:1, March 2000.

Barber, William J. "Reconfigurations in American Academic Economics: A General Practitioner's Perspective." In Bender, Thomas and Carl E. Schorske, eds. *American Academic Culture in Transformation: Fifty Years, Four Disciplines*. Princeton: Princeton University Press, 1997.

Beck, Paul A., et al. "Planning Our Future: The Report of the American Political Science Association's Strategic Planning Committee." *PS: Political Science and Politics* 33:4 (December 2000).

Bender, Thomas. "Politics, Intellect, and the American University, 1945–1995." In Thomas Bender, Thomas and Carl E. Schorske, eds. *American Academic Culture in Transformation*.

————. *Intellect and Public Life: Essays on the Social History of Academic Intellectuals in the United States*. Baltimore: Johns Hopkins University press, 1993.

Bender, Thomas and Carl E. Schorske, eds. *American Academic Culture in Transformation: Fifty Years, Four Disciplines*. Princeton: Princeton University Press, 1997.

Block, David. *Assessing Scholarly Communication in the Developing World: It takes More Than Bytes*, SSRC Working Paper Series on Building Intellectual Capacity for the 21st Century. New York: SSRC, 2001.

Bollag, Burton. "An African Success Story at the U. of Dar es Salaam." *The Chronicle of Higher Education* April 6, 2001.

————. Chaos on African Campuses." *The Chronicle of Higher Education* July 12, 2002.

Bourdieu, Pierre. "The Peculiar History of Scientific Reason." *Sociological Forum* 6:1, 1991.

Brooks, Stephen and Alain-G. Gagnon, eds. *Social Scientists, Policy, and the State*. Westport, CT: Praeger, 1990.

———— eds. *The Political Influence of Ideas: Policy Communities and the Social Sciences*. Westport, CT: Praeger, 1994.

Brown, John Seely and Paul Duguid. *The Social Life of Information*. Boston: Harvard Business School Press, 2000.

Bud-Frierman, Lisa, ed. *Information Acumen: The Understanding and Use of Knowledge in Modern Business.* London: Routledge, 1994.

Caldwell, Richard A., ed. *Public Policy Resource Guide,* Denver: University of Denver Institute for Public Policy Studies, 2002.

Calhoun, Craig. "The Public Good as a Social and Cultural Project." In Walter W. Powell and Elisabeth S. Clemens. *Private Action and the Public Good.* New Haven: Yale University Press, 1998.

Carnevale, Dan. "World Bank Becomes a Player in Distance Education." *The Chronicle of Higher Education* December 8, 2000.

Chomsky, Noam et al. *The Cold War & the University: Toward an Intellectual History of the Postwar Years.* New York: The New Press, 1997.

Cohen, Arthur M. *The Shaping of American Higher Education: The Emergence and Growth of the Contemporary System.* San Francisco: Jossey-Bass Publishers, 1998.

Cohen, David. "The Worldwide Rise of Private Colleges." *The Chronicle of Higher Education*, March 9, 2001.

Cohen, Wesley M., Richard Florida, Lucien Randazzese, and John Walsh. "Industry and the Academy: Uneasy Partners in the Cause of Technological Advance" in Roger G. Noll, ed. *Challenges to Research Universities.* Washington: Brookings Institution Press, 1998.

Cohn, Bernard. "The Census, Social Structure, and Objectification in South Asia." In *An Anthropologist Among the Historians and other Essays.* Oxford: Oxford University Press, 1987.

Coleman, James S. *Policy Research in the Social Sciences.* Morristown, NJ: General learning Press, 1972.

Cordesman, Anthony. "Transitions in the Middle East." an address to the 8th US Mideast Policymakers Conference, September 9, 1999. Http://www.csis.org/mideast/reports/ transitions.html.

Crick, Bernard. *The American Science of Politics.* Berkeley: University of California Press 1959.

Crosby, Alfred W. *The Measure of Reality: Quantification and Western Society, 1250–1600,.* Cambridge: Cambridge University Press, 1997.

Dahl, Robert. *Democracy and its Critics*. New Haven: Yale University Pres, 1989.

Dennis, Michael Aaron. "Secrecy and Science Revisited: From Politics to Historical Practice and Back." In Judith Reppy, ed. *Secrecy and Knowledge Production*. Cornell Peace Studies Program, Occasional Paper #23, October 1999.

Desrosieres, Alain. "How to Make Things Which Hold Together: Social Science, Statistics, and the State." In Peter Wagner, et al., eds. *Discourses on Society*.

———. *The Politics of Large Numbers: A History of Statistical Reasoning*. Cambridge: Harvard University Press, 1998.

Dror, Yehezkel. *Design for Policy Sciences*. New York: Elsevier, 1971.

Easterbrook, Michael. "Murders and Threats Plague Colombia's Universities." *The Chronicle of Higher Education*, November 2, 2001.

Eberstadt, Nicholas. *The Tyranny of Numbers: Mismeasurement and Misrule*. Washington: The AEI Press, 1995.

El-Ghobashy, Mona. "The Case Against Saad Eddin Ibrahim Reveals Deep-Seated Suspicions About the Nature of Social Research." *Cairo Times* January 24, 2001.

Elshtain, Jean Bethke. "Why Public Intellectuals?" *The Wilson Quarterly*, 25: 4 (Autumn 2001).

Etzkowitz, Henry et al. "Academia, Interrupted: Normative Change in Science." Unpublished paper, 1998.

———, Andrew Webster, and Peter Healey, eds. *Capitalizing Knowledge: New Intersections of Industry and Academia*. Albany: State University of New York Press, 1998.

Evans, Peter. "The Eclipse of the State? Reflections on Stateness in an Era of Globalization." *World Politics* 50 (October 1997).

Featherman, David, and Maris A. Vinovskis, eds. *Social Science and Policy-Making: A Search for Relevance in the Twentieth Century*. Ann Arbor: University of Michigan, 2001.

Friedrich, Carl J. *Man and His Government*. New York: McGraw-Hill Book Co. 1963.

Gagnon, Alain-G. "The Influence of Social Scientists on Public Policy." In Brooks and Gagnon, eds. *Social Scientists, Policy, and the State.*

George, Alexander L. *Bridging the Gap: Theory and Practice in Foreign Policy.* Washington: United States Institute of Peace Press, 1993.

Giddens, Anthony. *The Nation-State and Violence.* Cambridge: Polity Press, 1985.

Graham, Hugh Davis, and Nancy Diamond. *The Rise of the American research Universities: Elites and Challengers in the Postwar Era.* Baltimore: Johns Hopkins University Press, 1997.

Gulbenkian Commission. *Open the Social Sciences; Report of the Gulbenkian Commission on Restructuring the Social Sciences.* Stanford: Stanford University Press, 1996.

Gunnell, John G.. "In Search of the State: Political Science as an Emerging Discipline in the U.S." In Peter Wagner, et al. eds. *Discourses on Society: The Shaping of the Social Sciences...* Guston, David H. *Between Science and Politics: Assuring Integrity and Productivity of Research.* Cambridge: Cambridge University Press, 1999.

Hale, Charles R. "What is Activist Research?" *Items and Issues,* Social Science Research Council 2:1–2 (Summer 2001).

Hall, Peter. "Policy Paradigms, Experts, and the State: The Case of Macroeconomic Policy-Making in Britain" in Brooks and Gagnon, eds. *Social Scientists, Policy, and the State...*

Halliday, Fred. "The Chimera of the 'International University.'" *International Affairs* 75:1 (1999).

Hardin, Russell et al. "Symposium (on the Future of Political Science)." *PS: Political Science and Politics* 35:2, June 2002.

Hedges, Chris "New Activists are Nurtured by Politicized Curriculums." *The New York Times* May 27, 2000.

Heginbotham, Stanley J. "The National Security Education Program." *Items,* Social Science Research Council 46:2–3, (June–September 1992.

Heilbron, Johan. "The Tripartite Division of French Social Science: A Long-Term Perspective." In Wagner, et al., eds. *Discourses on Society*.

Heineman, Robert A, William T. Bluhm, Steven A. Peterson, Edward N. Kearny. *The World of the Policy Analyst: Rationality, Values and Politics*. Chatham, NJ: Chatham House Publishers, 1997.

Held, David, Anthony McGrew, David Goldblatt, and Jonathan Perraton. *Global Transformations: Politics, Econommics, Culture*. Stanford: Stanford University Press, 1999.

Horowitz, Irving Louis, ed. *The Rise and Fall of Project Camelot*. Cambridge: MIT Press, 1967.

Hoxie, R Gordon. *A History of the Faculty of Political Science, Columbia University*. New York; Columbia University Press, 1955.

Huntington, Samuel P. *The Clash of Civilizations and the Remaking of the World Order*. New York: Simon and Schuster, 1996.

Jann, Werner. "From Policy Analysis to Political Management: An Outside Look at Public-Policy Training in the United States." In Wagner, et al., eds. *Social Sciences and Modern States*.

Katznelson, Ira. "The Subtle Politics of Developing Emergency: Political Science as Liberal Guardianship." In Chomsky, et al. *The Cold War and the University*. .

Keynes, John Maynard. *The General Theory of Employment, Interest and Money,* London: MacMillan, 1936.

Kramer, Martin. *Ivory Towers on Sand: The Failure of Middle Eastern Studies in America*. Washington, DC: The Washington Institute for Near East Policy, 2001.

Lasswell, Harold and Daniel Lerner. *The Policy Sciences: Recent Developments in Scope and Methods*. Stanford: Stanford University Press, 1951.

Lazarsfeld, Paul F. "The Policy Sciences Movement (An Outsider's View)." *Policy Sciences*, 6, 1975.

Lewontin, R. C. "The Cold War and the Transformation of the Academy." In Chomsky, et al. *The Cold War and the University*.

Lindblom, Charles E. "Political Science in the 1940s and 1950s." In Bender and Schorske, eds. *American Academic Culture in Transformation.*

————. and David K. Cohen. *Useable Knowledge: Social Science and Social Problem-Solving.* New Haven: Yale University Press, 1979.

Lindquist, Evert A. "The Third Community, Policy Inquiry, and Social Scientists." In Brooks and Gagnon, eds. *Social Scientists, Policy, and the State.* Lowen, Rebecca S., *Creating the Cold War University: The Transformation of Stanford* {Berkeley: University of California Press, 1997.

Lucas, Christopher J. *Crisis in the Academy: Rethinking Higher Education in America.* New York: St. Martin's Press, 1996.

Lupia, Arthur. "Evaluating Political Science Research: Information for Buyers and Sellers." *PS,* March 2000.

Mamdani, Mahmood. "Africa and African Studies." Unpublished manuscript, 2001.

Manicas, Peter. "The Social Science Disciplines: The American Model." In Wagner, et al., eds. *Discourses on Society.* .

Martinez-Eber, Valerie et al. In *PS: Political Science and Politics,* 34:4 (December 2000).

McCaughey, Robert A. *International Studies and Academic Enterprise: A Chapter in the Enclosure of American Learning.* New York: Columbia University Press 1984.

McDonald, Kim. "U.S. Dominates Nobel Prizes in Science, but All Its Winners Are Foreign Born." *The Chronicle of Higher Education,* October 22, 1999.

McGann, James G. and R. Kent Weaver, eds. *Think Tanks and Civil Societies: Catalysts for Ideas and Action.* New Brunswick: Transaction Publishers, 2000.

McMurtrie, Beth. "Foreign Enrollments Grow in the US, but So Does Competition from Other Nations." *The Chronicle of Higher Education,* November 6, 2001.

Menand, Louis. "Undisciplined." *The Wilson Quarterly*, 25:4, Autumn 2001.

Merkx, Gilbert W. "Area and International Studies and Its Stakeholders." In Neil J. Smelser and Paul J. Baltes. *International Encyclopedia of the Social and Behavioral Sciences*. Oxford: Elsevier Science Limited, 2001.

Merton, Robert K. "A Note on Science and Democracy." *Journal of Legal and Political Sociology* 1 (1942).

——. "The Role of the Intellectual in Public Bureaucracy." In *Social Theory and Social Structure* Revised edition. Glencoe: The Free Press, 1957) (first published in 1945).

——. The Matthew Effect in Science, II: Cumulative Advantage and the Symbolism of Intellectual Property." *ISIS* (1988).

——. "Our Sociological Vernacular." *Columbia: the Magazine of Columbia University*, November 1981.

Mill, John Stuart, *Some Unsettled Questions of Political Economy*. 1844.

Miller, D.W. " Middle East-Studies Programs Are Accused of Scholarly Orthodoxy." *The Chronicle of Higher Education*, October 26, 2001.

Miller, Roberta Balstead. "The Information Society: O Brave New World." *Social Science Computer Review* 13:2 (Summer 1995).

Mitchell, Timothy. "Fixing the Economy." *Cultural Studies* 12:1 (1998).

——. "The Middle East in the Past and Future of Social Science." In David Szanton, ed. *The Past and Future of Area Studies in the United States*. Berkeley: University of California Press, forthcoming.

Moberg, David. "Silencing Joseph Stiglitz." *Salon.com*, May 2, 2000, http://www.salon.com/news/feature/2000/05/02/stiglitz.

Moynihan, Daniel Patrick. *Maximum Feasible Misunderstanding: Community Action in the War on Poverty*. New York: The Free Press, 1970.

Muir, Edward. "They Blinded Me with Political Science: On the Use of Non Peer-Reviewed Research on Educatoin Policy." *PS: Political Science and Politics* 32:4 (December 1999).

Nathan, Andrew J. "Universalism: A Particularistic Account." In Lynda S. Bell, Andrew J. Nathan, and Ilan Peleg, eds. *Negotiating Culture and Human Rights*. New York: Columbia University Press, 2001.

Nathan, Richard P. *Social Science in Government: The Role of Policy Researchers,* new edition,. Albany: Rockefeller Institute Press, 2000.

Nelson, Robert H. "The Economics Profession and the Making of Public Policy." *Journal of Economic Literature* 25. March 1987.

Nelson, Richard, *The Moon and the Ghetto: An Essay on Public Policy Analysis*. New York: Norton, 1977.

Nettl, J. P. "The States as a Conceptual Variable." *World Politics* 20, 1968.

Noll, Roger M., ed. *Challenges to Research Universities*. Washington: Brookings Institution Press, 1998.

O'Meara, Patrick, Howard D. Mehlinger, and Roxanna Ma Newman, eds. *Changing Perspectives on International Education*. Bloomington: Indiana University Press, 2001.

Palattella, John. "May the Course Be With You: Universities Claim the Right to Sell Classes on the Internet. The Faculty Strikes Back." *Lingua Franca* March 2001.

Painter, Nell Irwin. "Black Studies, Black Professors, and the Struggles of Perception." *The Chronicle of Higher Education* December 15, 2000.

Pal, Leslie. "Knowledge, Power and Policy: Reflections on Foucault." In Brooks and Gagnon, eds. *Social Scientists, Policy, and the State*. New York: Praeger, 1990.

Powell, Walter W. and Elisabeth S. Clemens. *Private Action and the Public Good*. New Haven: Yale University Press, 1998.

Press, Eyal and Jennifer Washburn. "The Kept University." *The Atlantic Monthly* March 2000.

Prewitt, Kenneth, *Networks in International Capacity Building: Cases from Sub-Saharan Africa*. New York: SSRC, 1998.

———. "The Social Science Project: Then, Now and Next." *Items and Issues*, Social Science Research Council, 3:1–2 (Spring 2002).

Primack, Paul. "Private Gain, Public Loss: Why Policy Students Opt Out of Government Service." Working Paper 2, Rappaport Insitute for Greater Boston, John F. Kennedy School of Government, Harvard University, 2000.

Reuben, Julie A. *The Making of the Modern University: Intellectual Transformation and the Marginalization of Morality.* Chicago: University of Chicago Press, 1996.

Roelofs, Joan and Erkki Berndtson. "Foundations, Social Sciensts and Eastern Europe." In Brooks and Gagnon, eds. *The Political Influence of Ideas: Policy Communities and the Social Sciences.* Westport, CT: Praeger, 1994.

Ross, Dorothy, *The Origins of American Social Science.* Cambridge: Cambridge University Press, 1991.

Said, Edward, *Beyond the Academy: A Scholar's Obligations.* American Council of Learned Societies Occasional Paper, # 31, 1995.

Salamon, Lester M. et al. *Global Civil Society: Dimensions of the Nonprofit Sector,* Baltimore: The Johns Hopkins Center for Civil Society Studies, 1999.

Schiera, Pierangelo. "'Science and Politics' as a Political Factor: German and Italian Social Sciences in the Nineteenth Century." In Wagneret al. eds. *Discourses on Society.*

Schorske, Carl E. "The New Rigorism in the Human Sciences, 1940–1960." In Bender, and E. Schorske, eds. *American Academic Culture in Transformation.*

Scott, James C. *Seeing like a State: How Certain Schemes to Improve to Human Condition have Failed.* New Haven: Yale University Press, 1998.

Simpson, Christopher, ed. *Universities and Empire: Money and Politics in the Social Sciences during the Cold War.* New York: The New Press, 1998.

Singer, P. W. "Corporate Warriors: The Rise of the Privatized Military Industry and Its Ramifications for International Security." *International Security* (Winter 2001–01).

Skowronek, Stephen. *Building a New American State: The Expansion of National Administrative Capabilities, 1877–1920.*. New York: Cambridge University Press, 1982.

Slaughter, Sheila and Larry L. Leslie. *Academic Capitalism: Politics, Policies and the Entrepreneurial University.* Baltimore: Johns Hopkins University Press, 1997.

Smith, James Allen. *Brookings at Seventy-Five* Washington, DC: The Brookings Institution, 1991.

Solow, Robert M. "How Did Economics Get That Way and What Way Did It Get?" In Bender, Thomas and Carl E. Schorske, eds. *American Academic Culture in Transformation: Fifty Years, Four Disciplines.* Princeton: Princeton University Press, 1997.

Sorauf, Frank et al. "Political Science at the NSF: The Report of a Committee of the American Political Science Association." *PS: Political Science and Politics* 33:4, December 2000.

Stone, Diane. *Capturing the Political Imagination: Think Tanks and Policy Processes,* London: Frank Cass, 1996.

Stiglitz, Joseph E. "Whither Reform? Ten Years of Transition." Keynote address for the World Bank Annual Conference on Development Economics, Washington DC, April 28–30, 1999.

——. *Globalization and Its Discontents.* New York: Norton, 2002.

Tesner, Sandrine, with the collaboration of Georg Kell. *The United Nations and Business: A Partnership Recovered.* New York: St. Martin's, 2000.

Tribe, Laurence. "Policy Sciences: Analysis or Ideology." *Journal of Philosophy and Public Affairs* 2. 1972.

Theodoulou, Stella Z. and Matthew A. Cahn, eds. *Public Policy: the Essential Readings.* Englewood Cliffs: Prentice-Hall, 1995.

UNESCO. *World Social Science Report 1999.* Paris: UNESCO/Elsevier, 1999.

Veysey, Lawrence R. *The Emergence of the American University.* Chicago: University of Chicago Press, 1965.

Vitalis, Robert. "The Graceful and Generous Liberal Gesture: Making Racism Invisible in American International Relations." *Millenium: Journal of International Studies*, 29:2, 2000.

————. "International Studies in America." unpublished paper, 2002.

Vout, Malcolm. "Oxford and the Emergence of Political Science in England, 1945–1960." In Wagner et al., eds. *Discourses on Society*.

Waechter, Bernd. "European Universities Must Adapt in an Era of Global Competition." *The Chronicle of Higher Education*, December 7, 2001.

Wagner, Peter, Carol Hirschon Weiss, Bjorn Wittrock, and Helmut Wollman, eds. *Social Sciences and Modern States: National Experiences and Theoretical Crossroads*. Cambridge: Cambridge University, Press 1991.

Wagner, Peter, Bjorn Wittrock, and Richard Whitley, eds. *Discourses on Society: The Shaping of the Social Sciences*. In *Sociology of the Sciences: A Yearbook*, vol. 15.. London: Kluwer Academic Publishers, 1991.

Wagner, Peter and Bjorn Wittrock. "States, Institutions, and Discourses: A Comparative Perspective on the Structuration of the Social Sciences." In Wagner et al., eds. *Discourses on Society*.

Waldo, Dwight. *The Administrative State: A Study of the Political Theory of American Public Administration*. New York: The Ronald Press, 1948.

Wallerstein, Immanuel. "The Unintended Consequences of Cold War Area Studies." In Chomsky, et al. *The Cold War and the University*.

Weaver, Mary Anne. "Egypt on Trial" *The New York Times Magazine*, June 17, 2001.

Webster, Andrew and Henry Etzkowitz. "Toward a Theorietical Analysis of Academic-Industry Collaboration." In Etzkowitz et al., eds. *Capitalizing Knowledge: New Intersections of Industry and Academia*. Albany: State University of New York Press, 1998.

————. *The End of the World as We Know It: Social Science for the Twenty-first Century*. Minneapolis: University of Minnesota Press, 1999.

Weintraub, E. Roy. *How Economics Became a Mathematical Science*, Durham: Duke University Press, 2002.

Weiss Carol, 1990. "The Uneasy Partnership Endures: Social Science and Government." In Brooks and Gagnon, eds. *Social Sciences, Policy, and the State.*

Whitaker, Brian. "US Thinktanks Give Lessons in Foreign Policy." *The Guardian*, August 19 2002.

Whitley, Richard. *The Intellectual and Social Organization of the Sciences* 2nd edition. Oxford: Oxford University Press, 2000.

Willinsky, John. *Learning to Divide the World: Education at Empire's End*. Minneapolis, MN: University of Minnesota Press, 1998.

Wilson, Woodrow. "The Study of Administration." *Political Science Quarterly* II:2, June 1887.

Wittrock, Bjorn and Peter Wagner. "Social Science Developments: The Structuration of Discourse in the Social Sciences." In Brooks and Gagnon, eds. *Social Scientists, Policy, and the State.*

World Bank. *Claiming the Future: Choosing Prosperity in the Middle East and North Africa*. Washington, DC, 1995.

Worcester, Kenton W. *The Social Science Research Council, 1923–1998*. New York: Social Science Research Council, 2001.

Ziderman, Adrian and Douglas Albrecht. *Financing Universities in Developing Countries*. Washington: The Palmer Press, 1995.

Ziman, John. *Real Science: What It Is, and What It Means*. Cambridge: Cambridge University Press, 2000.

Index

academic culture, 70–71
accountability, in public
    policy, 11
accounting firms, 59–60
Acheson, Dean, 117 n.51
activist research, 68
administrative culture, 125 n.64
advertisers, 51–52
advocacy, 60, 65–68
Africa, 78, 84, 86, 87–88
African-American studies, 69
Al Gohari, Mohammed, 101
America. *See* United States
American Economic
    Association, 16, 91

American English, 70
American Enterprise
    Institute, 46
American Federation of
    Teachers, 67
American Journal of
    Sociology, 17
American Political Science
    Association (APSA), 18,
    56–57, 59, 99–100
American Political Science
    Review, The, 18
American Social Science
    Association (ASSA),
    15, 16

Index compiled by Fred Leise

Calhoun, Craig, 38, 72, 106
Campaign to Ban
    Landmines, 48
Canada, 63
Carnegie Foundation, 25,
    26, 29
Census, U.S. Bureau of the, 19
Central Asia, 99
Central Europe, 87
charitable organizations, 24;
    See also private sector,
    private foundations
Chevron, 53
childcare facilities,
    nonprofit, 46
Citigroup, 53
CODESRIA (Council for the
    Development of Social
    Research in Africa), 87–88
Cole, Juan, 47
collaboration, 61–62
college degrees, numbers of,
    121 n.17
colleges. *See* land grant
    colleges; universities
Columbia University; Faculty
    of Political Science, 22;
    Graduate Program in
    Public Affairs, 7–8; prewar
    influence, 33; Russian
    Institute, 93; School of
    International Affairs,
    92–93; School of
    International and Public

Affairs, 2–3, 36; School of
    Political Science, 15–16;
    social science research
    funding, 29
commercialization of social
    sciences, 55
Committee on Political
    Development (Social
    Science Research
    Council), 94
common good. *See* public good
communism (communality),
    61–65, 106–107
communism (political
    movement), 94–95,
    96–97, 98
Comparative Politics section
    (American Political Science
    Association), 99–100
Comte, Auguste, 12
consulting companies, 59–60
context, in area studies,
    importance of, 97–102
Cordesman, Anthony, 11
corporate social
    responsibility, 45
corporations, 44, 45, 54
Council for the Development of
    Social Research in Africa
    (CODESRIA), 87–88
Council of Economic
    Advisors, 28
Council on Foreign
    Relations, 46

cultural studies, 38

Dahl, Robert, 116 n.42
data, social and economic, 50
data archives, large-scale, 79
democratization of social
    sciences, 50–61
demographers, professional, 19
Dennis, Michael Aaron, 63
dependency theory, 67, 95–96
Desrosieres, Alain, 9, 26–27
developing countries, 45
development, National Science
    Foundation on, 13
development theory, 94–95
Dewey, John, 116 n.44, 15
diploma mills, 49
disciplinary boundaries,
    37–38, 53
doctoral degrees, 79

East Asia, 85, 86–87
Eastern Europe, 85, 86, 87
*Ecole libre des sciences
    politiques,* 21
economics; focus of, shift in,
    16–17, 32–33; Hall on, 12;
    laws of, nonuniversality of,
    114 n.24; neoclassical
    approaches, 98; PhD
    holders' nationalities, 79
economists, 55–56, 112 n.3,
    114 n.24

Eder, Richard, 113 n.11
education. *See* higher
    education; universities
education, secular, 13
Egypt, 89, 100–101
Eisenhower, Dwight D., 30
El-Ghobashy, Mona, 100–101,
    130 n.53
Elshtain, Jean Bethke, 15
empirical research, 82
employment market, 33, 55;
    See also social scientists,
    employment
England, 22; *See also* Britain
Etzkowitz, Henry, 56, 68
Europe; Americanization,
    resistance to, 77; higher
    education, 49–50; political
    science, 22; social science
    debates, effects of, 78;
    socialism, 14; state, impor-
    tance of, 20–21; universities,
    conservatism, 14, 22, 82; *See
    also* Eastern Europe;
    France; Germany; Western
    Europe
European Higher Education
    Area, 49–50
Evans, Paul, 63
Evans, Peter, 65
expertise, technocratic, 19

Fabian Society, 114 n.22

higher education *(continued)*
participation in, 121 n.17;
purpose of, American views
on, 14; social sciences
spending, 78; state support
of, 83; *See also* universities
history; appropriation of, 80;
importance, 96; social
sciences and, 18
Hollander, Jacob, 91
Home Depot, 44
hospitals, nonprofit, 46
House of Representatives, 97
Hudson Institute, 46
human behavior, 38
Human Rights Watch, 48, 60
humanities, social function, 34
Hurewitz, J. C., 93

Ibn Khaldun Center for
Development Studies, 100
Ibrahim, Saadeddin, 100,
130 n.53
identity politics, 71–72
IMF (International Monetary
Fund), 44, 99
imperialism, 91
indeterminacy of social
sciences, 23–24
India, 54, 84
information, 9, 66–67, 70
information society, 83
Institute for Policy
Studies, 46

Institute for Public Policy
Studies (University of
Denver), 66
intellectual property rights,
64–65
intellectuals, 8
interdisciplinary research, 105
International Association for
the Study of Persian-
speaking Societies, 81
International Monetary Fund
(IMF), 44, 99
international students, 79
international studies academics,
118 n.59
International Training and
Research program (Ford
Foundation), 93
internationalization of public
policy practice, 4
IQ tests, 20
Iran, 85
Iraq, 89

Jann, Werner, 35, 36, 71
Jenks, J. W., 91
Johns Hopkins University,
The, 15
Johnson, Lyndon, 30
*Journal of Race
Development,* 20

Katznelson, Ira, 28
Kazakhstan, 53

Kennedy, John F., 30
Kennedy School of
Government, 36, 37
Keynes, John Maynard, 112 n.3
Kirk, Grayson, 93
knowledge, growing demand
for, 84
knowledge-based industries,
59–60
knowledge economy, 64
Koc University, 84

labor unions, 59
land grant colleges, 13
language, 70
Lasswell, Harold, 23, 30
Latin America; higher
education funding, 84;
political science, 99–100;
private universities, 85;
social science, influence of,
95; social science
communities, 86; social
scientists, role of, 105
Laura Spelman Rockefeller
Memorial, 25
Lazarsfeld, Paul, 32, 33
liberal institutions,
American, 72
liberal politics, 100
liberalism; American, 6,
107–108; influence, 8, 41;
public good and, 76;
sciences and, 13; social

science, association with,
88, 108; state, skepticism of,
39; in Western Europe,
81–82
Libya, 89
Lindblom, Charles, 72, 119 n.69
Lindquist, Evert, 65
Lipsky, Martin, 37
local, global vs., 104
local knowledge, 61
London School of Economics,
77, 114 n.22
Lupia, Arthur, 54–55

MacNamara, Robert, 117 n.56
Manhattan Project, 28
Marburger, John, 58
market and marketability, 39,
43–50, 54–55
marketization, 43–44, 49
McCaughey, Robert, 96, 118
n.59
Mead, Margaret, 33
media, 59, 90
media empires, 70
MENA (Middle East and North
Africa) region, 44
Merck, 44
Merton, Robert; on
intellectuals and policy
makers, 8; on public policy
and universalism, 68; on
science, communality in,
61; on science, ethos of, 60;

Merton, Robert *(continued)*
  on science, property in, 62;
  on social science, indeterminacy of, 23–24; on sociology,
  dominance of, 33
methodological
  individualism, 14
Middle East, 11, 47, 106,
  128 n.34
Middle East and North Africa
  (MENA) region, 44
Middle Eastern studies, 95
Mill. J. S., 12
Miller, Roberta, 79, 83
Mitchell, Timothy, 27, 67
modern state. *See* state
  (political unit), modern
modernization theory
  (development theory),
  94–95
Moley, Raymond, 26
moral improvement, 15, 19
morality, 70
Moscos School of Social
  Sciences, 84
Mosely, Philip, 93
Muslim countries, 88, 89

Nathan, Andrew J., 101
nation-states, 27
National Bureau of Economic
  Research, 25, 46
National Council of Charities
  and Corrections, 16

National Defense Education
  Act, Title VI, 94
National Science Foundation,
  13, 28, 57
National Security Education
  Program, 122 n.29
national university systems, 78
natural sciences, 12–13
Navy (U.S.), 92
Nazism, 28, 95
New School for Social
  Research, 116 n.44
New York City, 1–2
New York Times, The, 67
news organizations, 67; *See
  also* media
newspapers, 51
NGOs. *See* nongovernmental
  organizations
Nobel Peace Prize, 48
nongovernmental organizations
  (NGOs), 45–46, 48, 84,
  85–86
not-for-profit organizations,
  45–46

Oakeshott, Michael, 77
objectivity, 66
Office of Strategic Services, 92
outsourcing, 49

Painter, Nell, 69
Pal, Leslie, 31, 50–51
particularism, 70–71

passport holders, in U.S. House
of Representatives, 97
patents, 64
peer review, 33, 61
Pentagon, 117 n.56
perestroika, 44
Philippines, 91
philosophers, 9
PMFs (private military
firms), 45
Polanyi, Michael, 69
policy; definition of, 112 n.8;
public (*See* public policy);
ubiquity, 10
policy activists, 71–72
policy inquiry, 65
policy science, 30, 32
political advocacy, 66
political analysis, 36
political economy, 16, 17
political philosophers, 112 n.3
political process, 99
political science, 17, 22, 57–58,
98–99, 100
Political Science Quarterly, 22
political scientists, 37
political units. *See* nation-states;
state
politics, 7–40, 37, 109; *See also*
identity politics
Poverty, War on, 104
Powell, Walter, 10
power, 3, 106, 107
presentism, 80

Prewitt, Kenneth, 90
Primack, Paul, 48–49
private sector; private
businesses, 84; private
foundations, 24–25, 29, 35,
42, 93; private funding of
social science research,
85–87; private military
firms (PMFs), 45; as
public policy locus, 4
private universities, 49, 84
privatization, 4, 5, 45–46
products, value of, 54–55
professional associations,
56–59, 97
Project Camelot, 32
property, 61–65
proprietary research, 62
pseudo-universalism, 80
public, the, 106
public administration, 35
public good; Calhoun on, 72;
definition of, locus of, 104;
liberal commitment of, 76;
moral responsibility for,
110; origins of, 38–39;
public policy elites and,
116 n.42; universalism and,
69, 70
public policy; area studies
scholars and, 96–97; autocratic governments' views
on, 89; differing bases for,
88–89; engine of, 43–50;

public policy *(continued)*
environment of, changes in,
106; Europe, social science
influence on, 82; failures,
lessons of, 99; locus of, 4,
11, 53; marketization of,
43–44, 76; National Science
Foundation and, 58; origin,
sectoral, 10–11; political
environment, 36; politics as
element of, 109; practitioners
of, social scientists and, 2;
research and, 63, 82–83;
research as requirement for,
82–83; scientific, 7–40; social
science, global acceptance
of, 81; social science, relationship between, in twenty
first century, 106–107, 108;
state, association with, 10;
technocratic approach to,
104; training on, in United
States, 82; in twenty-first
century, 103–110; *See also*
public policy schools; public
policymakers
public policy analysts, 65–66, 72
public policy elites, 116 n.42
"Public Policy Resource
Guide" (Institute for Public
Policy Studies, University
of Denver), 66
public policy schools, 26–40,
35–38, 71, 109, 125 n.64

public policymakers, 8, 97,
109–110, 127 n.18
Puerto Rico, 91

quantitative sociology, 27

race, 20
RAND Corporation, 46
Reagan, Ronald, 43
religious instruction, 14–15
reputational systems, 64
research, 28, 62–63, 68,
82–83, 105; *See also* social
research; social science
research
research enterprise, 19–24
research universities, 41–42
Robinson, Geroid, 93
Rockefeller Foundation, 26,
29, 93
Roosevelt, Theodore, 15
Rostow, Walt, 94
royal academies, 11
Russell Sage Foundation, 25
Russia, 87, 89, 99; *See also*
Soviet Union
Russian Institute (Columbia
University), 93

Said, Edward, 34–35
Saudi Arabia, 89
School of International Affairs
(Columbia University),
92–93

School of International and
Public Affairs (Columbia
University), 2–3, 36
School of Military Government
and Administration (U.S.
Navy), 92–93
schools of public policy. *See*
public policy schools
science(s); American
universities, growth of, and,
14–19; basic, 28; definition
of, 113 n.11; early modern,
locus of, 11; liberalism and,
13; modern ethos of, 60; *See
also* political science; social
science
scientific knowledge, 61
scientific methods, 89
scientific research, 28, 83
scientists, 69
Scott, James, 9, 10, 37, 61,
68–69
secret research, 62–63
secular education, 13
September 11 terrorist attacks,
1–2
Singer, P. W., 45
skepticism, 65–68, 72
Skrowonek, Stephen, 112 n.4
Small, Albion, 17
social conflict theory, 32
social reform movements, 17
social research, 14, 17; *See also*
social science research

social researchers, European,
20–21
social responsibility,
corporate, 45
social science(s); across-
borders collaboration, 79;
advocacy and skepticism in,
65–68; communism of, end
of, 61–65; democratization
of, 50–61, 67–68; development of, 3; disciplinary
chauvinism, 37–38; dual
commitment, 72, 73; globalization of, 77–81; influence,
23; liberalism, association
with, 88, 89, 90; marketability, 54–55; natural sciences,
relationship to, 12–13; orienting axes of, 103; parochialism, 105; public accountability, removal from, 103;
public policy, as basis for,
81; as research enterprise,
19–24; retreat of, 1960s and
1970s, 31–35; skepticism
in, 65–68; support for, as
political act, 89; in twenty-
first century, 103–110;
universalism in, 68–73,
90–92, 97–102; universities,
retreat to, 26–40
social science, American;
characteristics, 88, 90;
foreign practice of, 81;

University of California, Berkeley, 29, 36
University of Chicago, The, 15
University of Denver, 66
U.S. Army, 92
U.S. Bureau of the Census, 19
U.S. Department of the Army, 32
U.S. House of Representatives, 97
U.S. National Science Foundation, 13
U.S. Navy, 92

Veblen, Thorstein, 116 n.44
Venezuela, 53
Vietnam War, 104
Vitalis, Robert, 20

Waechter, Bernd, 50
Wal-Mart, 44
Walker, Francis, 13
Wallace, Andrew, 56
Wallace, George, 31
Wallace, Schuyler, 92–93
War on Poverty, 104
War on Vietnam, 104
war zones, 128 n.30
Washington Consensus, 44, 98
Washington Institute for Near East Policy (WINEP), 47
webs, 79

Weintraub, E. Roy, 32–33
Weiss, Carol, 127 n.18
welfare state, 25, 42
Western Europe, 81–83
White House Council of Economic Advisors, 28
Whitley, Richard; on economics PhDs, job market for, 119 n.64; on intellectual obsolescence, 23; on reputational systems in private firms, 64; on social science research, American model of, 39; on social science research, funding for, 60; on social science research, globalization of, 80; on social science stakeholders, 12; on sociologists, distinctive competencies of, 52–53
Willensky, John, 91
Wilson, Woodrow, 16, 19, 22
WINEP (Washington Institute for Near East Policy), 47
Wolin, Sheldon, 23
women's studies, 69
Wood, Bryce, 93
Worcester, Kent, 25
World Bank, 44
World War I, 20
World War II, 27, 28

refs for thesis
92 intwr pd ^{us} ss little int m wld affairs
→but why not? obscured 'Am' project? abstract
pub gen
103-4 distanced, pub /Amer good and reventrance
see major 104 arg

Ch 4 cont'd
  US cs encouraged by Fall of comnsm
  to apply their anlyt models to new
  regions. IMF WB policy failures
    w/in 10yrs
  Some late 90s / now discuss why 100-1

Concl Ch 5

      quick runby of ss hist 103-4
A: - defining social and public, p good less
    in cntrol of state 104m
    mult sites of this + for rule of ss 104b
     ID work for 105+

LA chais sitn now: 106mb ; and re-a of maun arg
  truth and power 106 (and later)
LA: one chall for ss 106
    Common of sci commnty giving way to lib pluralism
  paroch → cosmopol tnsm 107m   107

     univsts still site for minor 108b
      `and pol sch's   curric chgs 109

   Some norm-a's: 107,8,9
        comna
          good

               another lib
               def 107

Ch 4
pub-engag 75
in 60s

60s private, particular
knowl rises
lib goals for pub good recedes
76 n

n-s challenge 77 t
↳ forces allow to soc sci and pub pol
post WW2 is when US ed model becomes infl+l in Europe
90s - study of foreigners ass was cold war idea; now collap 79
    - int'ntl g students in US 79; also studies abroad int'ntl 79
    - attempts to ustd famls in ufam, regionality ingl ed uds
U.S. area studies comm 80b
    - actors for whom sc∞ pub pol was imp in 90s/turn c
       and where ss not imp - lack of lib values and growth
    - Eur ed arrangements post WW2 82 81 of stat
       i - state collected data, then own ss analyzed 82
where higher ed didn't see much support 4/ e. 80s
state, policy co ss was much weaker 83 (compare
    - declin/failed state support Af, LAm, India Iran welfare collapse)
       → NGO private need steps in 80s/90s p 84 priv uys
* nexus of instit'ng 85 m
   85b — yet challenges for sustng natl. in community
                ↳ (ties to private by LA)
              86 - contrast LAm w/ E Eur etc
        or priv & f/ outside n m - nonlocal ss agenda 86
            also employ pool effect 86   Afr
         topic/methods/resources 87

LA's char of Am SS lib ism — 88 t
   all apprchs to pub pol (non SS) 88-9   w'eyn l.l
   autocrat leaders more census of ss lib ism than 55/s 89
      parochialism + structing of W ss's univ'ism 90-1
   anthro espec and int'l rus'roost 91-2
   Cold War science guise frspying 92
   intl war pol us little intrst in world affairs 92
   as US rose to world power post WW2, area
      studies emerges to learn about the het new
            (see 90 IR + AS)
   92-3 / ↳ war effort OSS etc; 40s-60s prvfound'ns
         55's cited fears of overspec + paroch 93 too
        ↳ Title VI of NDEA 1959 I, univ AS 94 (communist too
   94 modern zt'n/ development theory (alt to cmnst theory) fears)
      AS ppl in 60s → 90s alienated by lack of
         gov't/policy/ss attn to cult/regnl diffs,
         loss of purpose 96-7

Ch 3   the priv stuch (see 73)   41-3 ~ sum of ch 2

pub/priv and lib'ism 41
    and n-s (and us infl.) and F $

lib 43m   60s moral-p63   1920s l.L ag'. then 70s +6
                                    See WS under IR

arketiztn of pub pol' 43m 76   55 democratised
    market best diffuses values 43 6-44   see 53 and
            Reag goals that   earlier
    gov't recedes   67b
    market - gov't - UN - dev wld ch go 44-5
                                        NGO

IR   think tanks vs univ. med expos, methods 49
        around world 48
        multi v b ty 53   newsprs
        n-s, non gov actors 53   and lang b
        polisci in 90s. declinisig. NSF struggle,   55 51
        charity status. market orntn 56 to 9   ss and stats as
            NGO industi employ 59-60   part of pub fro c
        -Secrecy, gov't sponsored research   51-2
        area studies. US action 62-3
        knowl economy 64   [corp finance of
        policy analysts 65 & outside discipline 72   univ vs 54
        all policy knowl is spun '66 no peer review   prop rights 55
        SSRC activist research 2001-68   ps chnd journ ishe
    WS and AAS response to failure of lib Canada in   es neg by NSF
        also * 70mm dom of US acad prv sci sel 57
    loc of anti/trust; pol schools in world a cad 70t intell prop is
                                        in that   secured thru
    public good 64, 63, 69, 70+71L   conflict   giving away/
                                          70-1   making public
                                        and polans 72   62

                                                    then n-s?
                                                    124 n 49

    issues ongoing policy, actors' practice   Am pub pol schools
    are pub good ownership norm/moral stance   not pwrp to address
    as ident or int of self or others   dilemmas of
    market/gov't shiftg relate to univ   welf state 71m
        NGO pol analysts new actors

refs pt in thesis 42 f
        relat'd 69m - state mediator btwn sci policy
            II wl any period 72 m (also 74m
        i see p 90 m ss proj has been   departure of state
                        America   encouraged knowl
                                        as property moves

n-s less important 4m
the public 4, 6th, 10m ~24 ~29

global, priv z'm 4
level of soc sci 3m, 5m (post 9-11 and prior), 56-64   welfare
persp on CM 3 16 22 29 , 30   state,
          22 92   *Europe   state + public,
                            v US /4   glob dissem
IR 9+ 30 31n59 33 34 36 39   (indiv,
                              socism,
                              capit)

ideas of sci + gov't 9m 13m 18 19m 20 26 35 39
economics 19c early 20c nat US hist 15-6 → sociology 13,22m
moral progressive 18m, 25m44
   liberalism (+ private sector) 29 39 moralism 34 ss ambiv 34-5
state policy impt'and for Int war soc sci 20 25 z bn 47
public ____ 21-2, 29, 31, 32 - anti p-service '75 p admin 35 386
                                    396 p good market priv & govt
natl accounts 274, *29 n51
n-s in interwar period 27m
  23m US, world (intell reorg)
devel nat sci 28m   German univ
                        v US org 33
                      rise US model 3 ?

FDR Brain Trust 26   WWL, pure research · Germans
bureaucr and soc scis in 26b   27-8 policy operational
welfare?   research-US
  state   govt
          one stone   Gr Dep. 26
          reluctance - 27b
                            indirect infl of fed $ on SS 29
post war many ss's released again   Project Camelot 32
  but C Econ Adv in '46   ss f/ war
Ss not in NSF, pure/applied 28
foundtns again
Pentagon revoltn 60s p30 then suspicion 36 b-1
                                Eisen
policy g schools 60s 70s ~75
lots more on policy us soc sci tensions (and lls to earlier c(e)d
   divisions) 34-37? separtn then overlap 38
Wash consensus, Reagan ere 39. new skept.
              slech 3 nts   of state, logic ?
                                    politics
                                    trust market
                                    to serve p good